Let God Arise

Let God Arise

Landmark's in Church History

MARCUS L. LOANE

CHRISTIAN
FOCUS

Copyright © Marcus Loane 2008

ISBN 978-1-84550-380-2

First published in
This edition published in 2008
by
Christian Focus Publications,
Geanies House, Fearn, Ross-shire,
IV20 1TW, Scotland, UK

www.christianfocus.com

Cover design by Daniel Van Straaten

Printed by CPD Wales

Contents

We have heard with our ears, O God,
And our fathers have told us.
What work thou didst in their days,
In the days of old.

Psalm 44:1 (RV)

Preface

Memory easily travels back over a little more than seventy years to the days when I had to translate the Latin text of the Venerable Bede's account of the origins of Church history in Northumbria. Even then, his record of Aidan and Oswald held a charm that one could hardly resist. The beauty and resonance of their lives of united devotion to the ever living Saviour have lost nothing of their appeal with the passing of time.

When I came to England for the first time some years later, I was to see Lindisfarne and Lutterworth, Cambridge and Oxford, Clapham and Durham, and to identify with them many whose names are now deservedly honoured in the story of our Christian heritage.

The chapters which follow were written at various intervals and for different purposes: there is no special sequence in the choice of subjects. They are hardly more than sketches, but they represent outstanding landmarks in the long perspective of history from the time of Aidan down to the end of the nineteenth century.

The choice of subjects is my own, and it leaps over many other land-marks which some may think of equal or superior importance. All too many people today want to treat the present without any regard for history or tradition. But while we do not want to live in the past, there is a sense in which the past always lives on in us. It is with this in mind that these sketches have been put together, and the book is a small tribute to those who have helped to make us what we are. It helps us as well to see what manner of men we ought to be.

1

Aidan
and
the Legacy of Lindisfarne

The story of Columba and Iona is almost legendary as the key to the spread of the gospel along the rugged coastline of western Scotland. Columba had already won renown as one who came of royal stock and whose birth had been foretold by Patrick himself. He was born on December 7th 521, near Lough Gartan in Donegal at a time when Ireland was famous for its learning and its monasteries. He studied at Clonard which was at the height of its fame under Finnian, and then taught at Glasnevin near Dublin until 544 when the school was broken up by the plague. This led him to return to the north where he entered upon a ministry that was to absorb all his energies. He began to travel throughout Ireland as teacher and evangelist, founding schools and monasteries. He was responsible for no less than thirty-seven monastic foundations, among them the House at Kells whose illuminated copy of the Gospels is now among the treasures of Trinity College Dublin. But the presence of so many saints and scholars in the Ireland of those far-off days was offset by the number of warring chieftains who kept the whole country in a state of turmoil. Columba himself was to become embroiled in one of these clan wars. This led to the Battle of Cooldreony in 561 when some three thousand men lost their lives. This in turn was to cause grievous trouble. He was censured by a Synod held at Teltown in Meath for the slaughter of so many who were pagans, without God and without hope in the world. He was told that he must go and win as many souls for God as had been lost on the field of battle. This left him with only one course to take; that was to go into voluntary exile somewhere out of sight from Ireland. Therefore in the early summer of 563, with twelve carefully chosen companions, he sailed from his beloved country, heading north towards the islands off the coast of Scotland. 'The tender, passionate, remorseful, sympathetic Irishman, a Celt of the Celts'¹ went out like Abraham, not knowing whither he went.

Columba and his companions landed in a tiny cove on the southern tip of Iona. The Port of the Coracle, as it is now called, is flanked by steep cliffs and must have looked grimly formidable. They climbed a small hill to search the sky-line for the coast of Ireland, but it was out of sight. All they could see was a bleak and rocky wasteland, but they set out for the north east where they found good pastures beneath an arc of hills. Here they settled, looking across a mile wide stretch of water to the Ross of Mull. Here the first church was built on a site just to the north of where the Abbey now stands. All that remains are a few rough stones of the cell in which Columba used to sleep on bare rock. It was inauspicious enough as a home for that small band of Irish exiles, but it was ideal for Columba. His reputation for saintliness and capacity for leadership were to transform Iona into an oasis of culture and worship in a largely hostile world. Columba's disciples were to travel throughout the Islands and Highlands; they were to plant outposts along the west coast of Scotland and as far north as the Shetlands, often in what seem like the most inaccessible and inhospitable places, rugged headlands lapped by the waves, and yet destined to become beacons of light in those dark and remote regions. Columba himself undertook many journeys by sea and land, planting churches and founding monasteries. For thirty-four years he was to remain at his chosen station, 'a spirit purified by the discipline of great sorrow'.[2] He came to be venerated by the whole Church; pilgrims found their way to Iona from all over Europe. At length, in June 597, only a few weeks after Augustine and his band of monks had landed at the Isle of Thanet, his life came to its close. He had transcribed the Psalms as far as the words: 'They that seek the Lord shall not want any good thing' (34: 10). He laid down his pen; 'here', he said, 'I must stop'. When the midnight bell summoned the brethren to the Chapel, they found him there. He raised his hand to give by sign the benediction he no longer had strength to pronounce, and so, like his Lord, passed away in the very act of blessing.

Iona was at its zenith at the time of Columba's death, but its most famous outreach still lay in the future. This was to be across the border in Northumbria. After the Battle of

Retford in 617 when Ethelfrid of Bernicia was slain, his son Oswald fled to Iona where he was housed and taught the faith of Christ. Then in 633 Edwin was slain in the Battle of Hatfield and the Kingdom of Northumbria fell apart once more into the sub-kingdoms of Deira and Bernicia. Their two rulers turned out to be worse than pagans and, in 634 at the age of thirty, Oswald, son of Ethelfrid and nephew of Edwin, resolved to fight for his kingdom. His small army was drawn up a few miles from Hexham on the rising ground to the north of the Roman wall. Early on that winter morning, he had a cross made and planted in the midst of his men; he called upon them to kneel down while he prayed for God's blessing; then he led them in a charge which overwhelmed the greatly superior enemy forces. This victory at Heavenfield allowed him to reunite Deira and Bernicia in a single kingdom as in the days of Edwin. Lightfoot observed that the ideal is that kings should be saints and that saints should be kings, but the combination is rare. Such a man was Alfred; such a man was Oswald: a true saint and a true king.[3] Oswald was to prove a truly able ruler, and yet was as devout as if he lived in a cloister. 'Strength and sweetness were united in a character which almost represents the ideal of Christian royalty.'[4]

His first and most urgent concern was to restore the work begun under Edwin and to bring his kingdom under wholesome Christian influence. He turned at once to that northern Celtic church which for years had been his home. At his request, a missionary was sent from Iona; 'but his first experience of (the) rude, indocile heathens (of Northumbria) drove him home again in hopeless disgust'.[5] He told his fellow monks that it was useless to attempt to convert such a stubborn people. One lone voice was raised in gentle remonstration: 'Brother, it seems to me that thou hast been unduly hard upon these untaught hearers, and hast not given them first according to the Apostle's precept the milk of less solid doctrine, until gradually nurtured on the Word of God, they should have strength to digest the more perfect lessons.'[6] All eyes were fixed on the speaker; this was Aidan. He was the man for such a task! So in 635 he was ordained and sent forth just as long before Barnabas and Saul were set apart by the laying on of hands and were sent forth to preach the gospel.

The gaunt headland of Bamburgh and the island of Lindisfarne jut out like twin sentinels into the North Sea from the coast of Northumbria. Oswald had his great rock fortress at Bamburgh, and Aidan chose Lindisfarne as the site for his monastic foundation. A stone causeway now provides access to the island when the tide is out; but for Aidan, it bore an irresistible resemblance to Iona. One may still stand among the ruins of the Priory, and look across the waters to Barnburgh, and dream of those halcyon days when Aidan and Oswald worked side by side in their efforts to make Northumbria a bright jewel in Christ's crown. Aidan's daily pattern of life was that of a monk, governed by the rules and habits in which he had been schooled at Iona. He had brought with him twelve fellow workers, and they were to him like Columba's companions; their heart was as his heart. He formed a school in which twelve boys were trained under his eye in the hope that one day they might preach to their own people. Sometimes he withdrew to the smaller islet of Farne about a mile and a half from shore; it gave him that solitude for the communion with God which was the strength and stay of his soul. Often

he travelled on the mainland, almost always on foot so
that he could meet and converse with rich and poor alike.
In his early journeys, he was accompanied by Oswald
whose knowledge of Aidan's Celtic tongue allowed him
to act as interpreter for his preaching. Lindisfarne and
Bamburgh were situated in Bernicia where the gospel had
been virtually unknown before the coming of Aidan and
Oswald. Bede was to say that the sight of the king and
the saint side by side as the gospel was being preached
was 'truly beautiful'. People flocked with eager delight to
hear the words of life; churches were built; children were
taught; and plots of ground were made available as sites
on which monasteries would rise. Aidan was an evangelist
of the finest type in his love for Christ and zeal for souls;
Oswald showed a depth of personal piety which marked
him out as another Josiah. Never did the pure flame of
true evangelism burn more brightly than in Oswald and
Aidan.[7]

It was acknowledged by the historian William Bright
that 'the history of the Church in Northumbria during
the larger part of the seventh century is conspicuously the
backbone of the history of the Church of England.'[8] The
history of Lindisfarne is undoubtedly the backbone of the
story of the gospel in Northumbria. It was totally separate
from the mission of Paulinus at York or of Wilfrid at
Hexham and Ripon. And its two great agents were Aidan
and Oswald who drew their strength neither from Rome
nor from Canterbury, but from the Celtic fountain at Iona.
But that glorious partnership between king and saint was
shattered in 642 when Oswald was slain by the heathen
Penda in the Battle of Maserfield. His last words as he fell
were words of prayer for his soldiers:

'O God, have mercy on their souls!'
'For bodies whatsoe'er betide,
On souls, O God, have mercy', cried
King Oswald, as he fell and died.[9]

The kingdom of Northumbria broke up again into the two regions of Deira and Bernicia. Oswald's younger brother, Oswy, took the northern kingdom, while his cousin, Oswin, was established in Deira. Oswin, like Oswald, was to provide 'a royal example of singular loveliness', and his character as sketched by Bede is one of Bede's finest portraits:

> In personal appearance tall and handsome, kindly in address, open-handed to gentle and simple, and withal, eminent for piety, he won the love of all by the royal dignity of his mind, his countenance, his conduct, so that from almost every province men of noblest birth flocked together to be thanes in the hall of Oswin of Deira.[10]

But the growing tension between the two kingdoms brought them to the brink of war in 651. Oswin was betrayed to Oswy and was put to death by Oswy's command. The two kingdoms of Deira and Bernicia were reunited under Oswy, but the death of Oswin was an irreparable loss. Aidan had been on the warmest terms of friendship with Oswin who was so like his greatly beloved Oswald, and the tragic circumstances in which Oswin had lost his life were not without effect in shortening Aidan's life as well. It was only some twelve days after Oswin's murder that he was staying at a royal villa near Bamburgh from which he had often set out on his preaching journeys. Illness overtook him so suddenly that his friends could only lay him on the ground near the west end of the church where his life ebbed quickly away. It was August 31st 651.

Aidan shines out in the records of that now far distant age as the most beautiful character of all the Scoto-Celtic school of saints. 'I know of no nobler type of the missionary spirit than Aidan', so Bishop Lightfoot declared.

> His character, as it appears through the haze of antiquity, is almost absolutely faultless. Doubtless this haze may have obscured some imperfections which a clearer atmosphere and a nearer view would have enabled us to detect. But we can not have been misled as to the main lineaments of the man.

And what were they? Leaving aside all that Bede has to say concerning miracles, and measuring him side by side with men like Wilfrid and Cuthbert, he stands before us with 'singular sweetness and breadth and sympathy of character. He had all the virtues of his Celtic race without any of its faults'.[11] All that was excellent in Columba could be found in Aidan; he too was 'tender, sympathetic, adventurous, self-sacrificing'.[12] But the grave faults which marred Columba's character were all wholly absent 'in the simple, wise, sympathetic, large-hearted, saintly Aidan'.[13]

Bede could not write about Aidan except in terms of glowing admiration. His gentleness, his sympathy, his sweetness and patience were matched by his discretion, his discipline, his simplicity and self-restraint. Many pilgrims were to visit the Holy Isle of Lindisfarne and were to leave generous gifts with Aidan. All such gifts were promptly used for the relief of the poor or for the ransom of those who had been sold as slaves. It was little wonder that he was known as the 'cherisher of the needy and father of the wretched'.[14] His long journeys on foot, his concern for evangelism and education, his friendship with Oswald and Oswin: all played their own part in making his name a legend during his own life-time. Cedd and Chad were among his disciples; Eata was one of his original twelve boys; Hilda was his fellow worker; Cuthbert was to wear his spiritual mantle. Lindisfarne was to become for England all that Iona was for Scotland. Lightfoot boldly summed it all up: 'Not Augustine, but Aidan, is the true Apostle of England'.[15]

Aidan's work was not to die with his death; a new bishop was sent from Iona to take his place. This was Finan; but good and godly though he was, he lacked those rare qualities of true saintliness which had been so conspicuous in the life of Aidan. He replaced Aidan's humble church building with one of hewn oak and thatched roof, and he refused to concede the historic tradition of Iona with regard to the proper date for Easter. But he did not possess Aidan's winning spirit, and his rough-edged temper was to exacerbate the whole issue in debate between the Celtic and Latin parties. A more memorable event took place with the baptism of Peada in 653; he was the son of the great heathen king, Penda of Mercia. This led to a major development: Finan chose four missionaries who returned with Peada to evangelize the Midlands. Two years later, for the third and last time, Penda led an army into Northumbria; he meant to crush Oswy once and for all as he had crushed Edwin and Oswald. But the Battle of Winwidfield on November 15th 655 saw the many scattered by the few, and Penda himself was slain.

Finan died in 661; Colman came in his place. He was 'a man of simple and austere piety, and an innate prudence which won Oswy's regard'.[16] He had to meet the great crisis of the Celtic mission when the Council of Whitby was convened in 664 to end the strife as to the right time for Easter. Colman had the support of Cedd and Hilda, but in the end Oswy succumbed to the imperious Wilfrid. Iona and its tradition were defeated; Lindisfarne as a Celtic mission was broken up. Colman withdrew to his Scottish home with a large group of Irish monks and scholars. This marked the end of the Celtic ascendancy; 'the age of Oswald and Aidan and Hilda was past'.[17] The next phase of the Church in Northumbria would bear a strong Latin impress. Nevertheless Bede who was yet to be nurtured in that Latin school would leave on record a fine testimony to the single-hearted goodness and pure unworldliness of those early Celtic leaders. The people of Northumbria had been made to feel what it was to be taught and cared for by men 'who before all things were the disciples and ministers of Christ, whose chief and type was a St. Aidan.'[18]

But there is more to tell. Two of Aidan's scholars had been the brothers Cedd and Chad. Cedd was one of the four missionaries sent to the Mid-Angles by Finan in 653 after the conversion of Peada. But he was soon recalled from that field of labour and sent instead to head a mission to the East Saxons. He traversed their kingdom, preaching the gospel, winning many converts, and building up a large church. In 654 he went back to Lindisfarne to confer with Finan and was consecrated as a bishop for the church in Essex. During the next ten years, he built churches, ordained fellow workers, and baptized converts on the banks of rivers such as the Thames. His monks were taught to observe the monastic life of Iona and Lindisfarne, and he founded the great monastery at Lastingham on one of his many visits to his native Northumbria. He acted as interpreter at the Council of Whitby to which he had come in support of Colman; but when Oswy ruled in favour of the Latin rule for Easter, Cedd agreed to conform. He went on from Whitby to visit Lastingham where he was stricken with the plague; he died before the year was out; it was 664.

Chad was destined to become even more famous. After Cedd's death, he was appointed the abbot of Lastingham: 'a holy man, grave in character,...a man of prayer, study, humility, purity, voluntary poverty'.[19] It was not long before Oswy prevailed upon him to become Bishop of York which had been left without a spiritual leader as a result of Wilfrid's prolonged absence in France. He was consecrated by the bishop of Wessex and two British bishops in 665: perhaps the first overt step towards a union of the British and English churches. His brief tenure of the See of York helped to mark him out as one of the truest saints of ancient England. He took pains to train his people on the pattern set by Aidan and Cedd, and he ruled the church as a whole in a manner which Bede felt was nothing short of sublime. Then in 669, he withdrew to Lastingham; but not for long. He was summoned once more to a wider ministry and was sent to Mercia where he settled at Lichfield. But his episcopate was all too brief. On March 2nd 672, he heard voices as of angels calling him home, and after receiving the Communion of the Body and Blood of Christ, he died with the vision of that heavenly home before his eyes. Cedd and Chad were Northumbrians by birth, and they were the spiritual offspring of Lindisfarne. It was through them that the Celtic mission founded by Aidan reached into Essex and the Midlands.

There is one more special post-script to the story of Lindisfarne; it is gathered round the name and life of Cuthbert. He was born in the year 631, or thereabouts, and grew up as a shepherd lad on the hills of Lammermoor. On the night of Aidan's death in August 651, he had a dream which he interpreted as a vision. As a result, he made up his mind to enter a monastery. For that purpose, he came to the Abbey at Old Melrose whose Abbot was Eata, one of Aidan's original scholars, and whose Prior was the learned Boisil. Cuthbert quickly surpassed all the brethren not only in manual labour, but also in studies, vigils and prayers. The years passed by until 664 when he succeeded Boisil as Prior and began to add to his other duties the work of an evangelist in the nearby Tweedside country. On foot or on horseback, he made his way into the wildest valleys, scaling the steepest hillsides, finding access to the poorest hamlets whose people had never before received such a visit.[20]

When Colman returned to Scotland after the Council of Whitby, Eata was appointed as Abbot of Lindisfarne in addition to his duties at Old Melrose and, in due course, Cuthbert was sent there as Prior to teach Aidan's rule of monastic perfection. His life among the brethren was itself a lesson on unwearied devotion, but was never strict enough for his own high ideal. At length, in 676, he gave up his duties as Prior in order to live as a recluse on the near-by islet of Farne to which Aidan used to retreat for solitude and communion with God. He built a round two-roomed hut, roofed with logs and straw; its walls were made of turf and stone; and from within he could see nothing but the sky. Nine years were spent in that self-imposed seclusion, and it acted on his nervous system much as it had done in the case of so many other hermits. From the perspective of a later period of time, he might seem less truly a saint during those years on Farne than when he was questing for souls in the valleys near Melrose or caring for monks at Lindisfarne; but his lowliness, his gentleness, his habitual brightness were not impaired by those years of solitary experience.[21]

In 684, Cuthbert was chosen as bishop of Hexham, and many envoys were sent to announce his election. But he would not move from his cell until the king himself, Egfrid, the son of Oswy, landed on Farne. Only then, and with tears in his eyes, did Cuthbert respond; but not without one special concession. It was arranged that Eata should go to Hexham while Cuthbert would become bishop of Lindisfarne. He was consecrated on Easter Day in March 685. 'And so the shepherd youth of Lammermoor, the scholar of Boisil, the evangelist of Tweedside, the Prior of Melrose, the hermit of Farne, began his short career as a bishop.'[22] Only a few weeks later, Egfrid was slain in the Battle of Dunnechtar near Forfar in Scotland, and his death brought to an end the long line of great Northumbrian kings. It would be long indeed before 'the crown of Edwin and Oswald resumed the majesty of their wide overlordship.'[23]

Cuthbert was seen as the man for the hour. He was Aidan's real heir in his single-minded unworldliness, though he differed from him in his recognition of and conformity to the Latin rule for Easter. He was just the same as before in lowliness and devotion, and his habits as an ascetic were to remain unaltered. He tried to go about as if he still had the energies of youth at his command, but his excessive austerities had in fact worn out his robust constitution. He made what proved to be a long farewell circuit of the churches under his care; then, after Christmas 686, conscious of failing strength, he returned to his solitary islet. But this, as the event would prove, was to prepare himself for death. At the end of February 687, his last illness came on. For five days a wild storm cut him off from all contact with Lindisfarne; he was alone except for the seabirds he loved. At length the monks landed on the little island once more, only to find that the end was at hand. On March 20th, Herefrid ministered to him the bread and wine as the pledges of redeeming love. Cuthbert lifted up his eyes and his hands; then, in Herefrid's words, 'sped forth his spirit into the joys of the heavenly kingdom'.[24] The sun which had risen and had shone so brightly with Aidan and Oswald was to set at last with the death of Egfrid and Cuthbert. But that span of time had been 'the golden age of saintliness, such as England would never see again'.[25]

For Further Reading

The Venerable Bede: *Ecclesiastical History of England*, edited by J.A. Giles, London, Bell, 1894.

William Bright: *Chapters of Early English Church History*, 1877.

J.B. Lightfoot: *Leaders of the Northern Church*.

2

John Wycliffe
and
The Early Lollards

When the long chase in The Hound of Heaven came
to an end, Francis Thompson still had to learn 'how
little worthy of any love thou art', and to hear God
ask: 'Whom wilt thou find to love ignoble thee, Save
Me, save only Me?'.

Francis Thompson: The Hound of Heaven

John Wycliffe has no equal in stature or prestige as scholar
and schoolman in the England of the fourteenth century.
He was born in 1320, or thereabout, in a Yorkshire hamlet
near Richmond. Nothing is known of his childhood, but in
due course he went up to Oxford. Here he was to remain for
the greater part of his life. Here he was to become the most
distinguished alumnus in an age when Oxford vied with

Paris for the premier position in the world of learning. He built up a splendid reputation as a theologian; he was for a time the Master of Balliol; and in 1372 he took his degree as a Doctor of Divinity. There was steady progress in the evolution of his thinking. His demand for disendowment came before his purely doctrinal heresies, and his quarrel with the friars before his rejection of transubstantiation. It is only in his later works that his main attack on the system as well as the doctrines of the mediaeval church is to be found in its developed form. It was his sheer brilliance that led him first into political activity, and then into the arena where suspicion of heresy overtook him.

Wycliffe was drawn into John of Gaunt's faction in 1374 and was appointed to the benefice of Lutterworth. John of Gaunt was to throw the mantle of his protection over Wycliffe during the next few years, and this was to prove invaluable when in 1377 the Pope issued a series of bulls to demand his arrest. The issues were political rather than doctrinal; they were based on his theory of the dominion of grace. He taught that all dominion or ownership was derived from God; those who disregarded the laws of God in Church or State should be *ipso facto* dispossessed of all dominion. He was seen as 'standing for England against Rome, for the State against the Church'.[26] But during 1379 and 1380, he ceased to be a central figure in the political conflict. He spent two quiet years in Oxford while he thought out the whole problem of transubstantiation. He was led to reject as absurd the idea of a miracle repeated many times a day, often by the lowest type of priest. But the Eucharist as distinct from the Mass was for him a mystery. The body was present in some manner, yet how he could not tell; he was only certain that the bread was still bread and as such was on the altar. It was when he began to teach these things that the break with John of Gaunt came about. In 1382, he was suspended from all his functions in Oxford and withdrew to Lutterworth. Lutterworth lay on the road between Oxford and Leicester where John of Gaunt had his seat. Wycliffe had passed freely to and from Lutterworth since his appointment in 1374, but had mainly resided in Oxford until his suspension in 1382. Lutterworth thereafter was his home until his death in 1384. It was during the last four years of his life that his great project for the translation of the Bible into English was conceived and begun. Wycliffe must have seen this project as the basis for the reform of Church and State; it was 'the practical measure to which his theories led him at the end of his life'.[27] The need for Church reform called for widespread knowledge of the Bible: this could not be achieved unless the Bible in English was made available for all who were able to read. It was his own knowledge of the Latin Vulgate which had led him to claim pre-eminence for the Bible as a spiritual authority. Mediaeval preachers had shown equal regard for the Vulgate and the Fathers. Wycliffe was 'the greatest English preacher of his day',[28] and it was 'his avowed object to make people attach more importance to the pulpit than to the Sacraments'.[29] He was ready to back his preaching from Vulgate and Fathers alike; when the Fathers did not agree with the Vulgate, he thought them of no value at all.

Hitherto no translation of the whole Bible into English had been made: the old Anglo-Saxon version was of small value in the fourteenth century. Wycliffe was to use every means in his power to provide a translation in current English and to promote its study by English men and women. 'His great merit was this, that he appealed from the Latin reading classes to the English speaking public.'[30] He had an eye for a wider reading public and lower social order than could be served by the Vulgate: first the knights; then the well-to-do merchants; and at length the rural classes. 'He was novel in insisting that simplicity of life could never be practised by the masses till they personally understood the Christianity of the Gospels and The Acts of the Apostles...All men needed to know 'Godde's Lawe'; all men needed...to follow Christ in His meek and poor and charitable living; and therefore all men as far as possible should have access to the written story of that life.'[31]

'In those days,' wrote Henry Knighton of 1382, 'flourished Master John Wycliffe, rector of the church of Lutterworth in the county of Leicester, the most eminent doctor of theology of those times. In philosophy he was reckoned second to none, and in scholastic learning without rival.'[32] But the storm that broke in Oxford after he was condemned in the course of that year effectively silenced the voice of his sympathisers in that city. Elsewhere a few Lollard preachers maintained their work, though in grave and growing peril. But while Wycliffe was no longer at the centre of learning in Oxford, he was as well able as ever to promote an accurate and scholarly translation of the Vulgate. Margaret Deansley has drawn attention to the direction of his thinking and the emphasis of his preaching as time went on. 'It is interesting,' she wrote, 'to trace in his written works between 1378 and his death in 1384 his efforts expressly to defend the value of the Bible as the final authority; to show that the people at large were ignorant of the gospel because of defective preaching; then that it was necessary for all, even the simplest, to know the Gospel so that they might follow Christ in meekness of living; then that the Gospels ought to be translated into English for this end; and finally that it was right that such translations had been made, though prelates raged against them.[33] Wycliffe himself may not have been responsible for more than a minor portion of the actual work of translation. The first version was in the main the work of the Lollard circle in Oxford. It was a literal translation of the Vulgate and it followed with a pedantic precision the word order of the Latin. This was clumsy, stilted, and quite unnatural in the English vernacular. But the second version which was largely the work of John Purvey was much freer in style, without any attempt to preserve the same word order as in the Latin. The General Prologue in its final form in 1395 contained a lucid statement of Purvey's aims and motives. 'At the beginning', he wrote, 'I purposed with God's help to make the sentence as true and open in English as it is in the Latin, or more true and more open than it is in the Latin...And whether I have done this or nay, no doubt they that con well the Scripture of Holy Writ and English together, and will travail with God's grace thereabouts, may make the Bible as true and open, yea, and openlier in English than it is in Latin.'[34]

There were no such aids for multiplying copies of the Bible as the printing press would afford a hundred years later. Wycliffe's Bible could only circulate in hand-written manuscript copies. Wycliffe himself was not content merely to secure a scholarly translation; he was just as concerned that the message of the Bible should reach ordinary people in their daily avocations. He had built up a band of 'poor' Lollard preachers who went out to travel round the village centres so that they could read the Bible aloud and teach people who as often as not were quite illiterate. The population of England was barely three million, and most people spent their lives in rural communities. It was to these people that the preaching of the Lollards appealed, and they eagerly responded to the attempt to set before them the gospel story in the language they used at home and work. They would instinctively appreciate Wycliffe's attack on tithes and his doctrine of evangelical poverty. They would rejoice in his criticism of papal claims and oppressive church demands. They could understand his rejection of the doctrine of transubstantiation as well as the fact that he still retained his reverence for the element of mystery in the Eucharist. They could understand his rejection of mediaeval ideas about the pardon of sin, though he never arrived at the doctrine of justification by faith only. They could easily understand why he was so vehemently opposed to prelates and friars. It is said that once when he was ill, the friars began to mock him as one who would soon be dead. But he staggered them by rising up and quoting the words of the Psalmist with an adaptation of his own: 'I shall not die, but live, and declare the evil works of the friars'. And live he did. He was hounded out of Oxford, but his last days in Lutterworth were undisturbed. He died peacefully on the last day of the year in 1384; it was only after his death that the Church took revenge. He was excommunicated; his body was exhumed; his bones were burnt; and the ashes were strewn on the waters of the Severn. But let Trevelyan have the last word. 'He was the herald of the Puritan movement, not only in its repudiation of ceremonies, but in the stern individual morality which it substituted;...and his life bears witness to the dauntless courage of a man who believes in his own immediate relation to God.'[35]

Wycliffe was dead; but the work which he had begun was to broaden in scope and strength through the labours of one particular devoted disciple. Most of Wycliffe's Oxford friends had fallen away as a result of the sudden storm of persecution in 1382; but John Purvey was to remain constant. It seems that he had been ordained to the priesthood about 1377 and had become Wycliffe's secretary. He took his Doctor's degree and won a reputation as a scholar who deserved the highest respect. The Carmelite Friar Thomas Walden was to speak of him as 'one of Wycliffe's followers, a man of great authority, and a most notable Doctor'.[36] He was only about thirty years old in 1382, too young perhaps to be caught up in the toils of persecution. But he withdrew from Oxford with Wycliffe and took up his residence with him at Lutterworth. He was Wycliffe's favourite disciple and intimate companion; he helped Wycliffe in his literary labours and drank deeply from the well of Wycliffe's teaching. And he caught up the torch Wycliffe had to lay down.

John Purvey was Wycliffe's spiritual legatee as well as his literary executor, and he stood out after 1384 as the designated leader of the Lollard movement. Henry Knighton was to describe him as grave in bearing, simple in dress, tireless in travel and preaching. 'As he strove to be an example of life and manners to the rest of his sect, so he imitated and conformed himself to the teaching of his master as an invincible disciple.'[37] This was the man who was mainly responsible for the second version of the English Bible during the ten years that followed Wycliffe's death. He expounded the principles which underlay the translation in the General Prologue which was written in 1395, and he made a noble appeal for the recognition of this version as an accurate translation. 'Let the Church of England', he wrote, 'now approve the translation of simple men that would, for no good on earth, by their writing and power, put away the least truth, the least letter or title of Holy Writ.'[38] Wycliffe's genius and Purvey's scholarship gave England the Bible for the first time in the language of the people.

Purvey withdrew to the west of England after 1384 in order to pursue his work on the Bible. There were Lollards in the court of Richard 11; Lollards in the circle of knights; Lollards in the poorer country classes. Sympathetic nobles like John of Gaunt were too strong in their own right for the Church to attack, but the Lollard preachers in the rural districts were subject to constant pressure. Purvey himself seems to have kept a low profile during the next few years after 1395, although London rather than Bristol had become his main centre. John of Gaunt died and Henry IV came to the throne in 1399. This turned out to be the prelude to a sustained attack on the Lollards. Purvey himself was caught in the mesh of this fresh persecution and was held in prison at Saltwood Castle until his trial took place in the Chapter House of St Paul's on the last day of February 1401. He was arraigned as a heretic and forced to make a public recantation at Paul's Cross on March 6th. William Thorpe held that his fortitude had been undermined by the privations he had endured while in Saltwood Castle.

Purvey was inducted to the vicarage of West Hythe in August 1401, but resigned in 1403. He seems to have gravitated between London and Oxford during the next few years, chiefly concerned with the defence of the English Bible. Then in 1407, Archbishop Arundel induced a provincial council at Oxford to pass thirteen resolutions with regard to Lollard activity. The first resolution prohibited preaching 'either in Latin or in the vulgar tongue' unless the preacher held a special license. This put an end to the Lollard in Oxford as well as to Purvey's struggle to uphold the lawfulness of his translations. After this, Purvey sank into obscurity. He seems to have been in prison between 1420 and 1426, and to have ended his days in prison or in hiding. William Thorpe, a Lollard, had met him in 1407 and had described him as one who 'sheweth himself to be neither hot nor cold'.[39] Margaret Deansley argued that he was a scholar whose breadth of view made for moderation and a capacity for seeing both sides of a question to his own undoing.[40] Purvey was more than a little like Cranmer as a man who recanted under threat of burning but who subsequenty returned to his faith at great risk to his own life.

Purvey's recantation must be seen in the light of two other factors. England had long been free from the more extreme forms of persecution which were common enough on the Continent. There was as yet nothing like a statutory authority for punishment of heresy with death; 'the heretic at the stake was a thing scarcely known in mediaeval England'.[41] Nevertheless the burning of various heretics across the Channel would be enough to stir up fears lest the same fate should be in store for the Lollards. And such fears were fulfilled as a result of the revolution which brought Henry IV to the throne. Henry had to depend on the clergy for much of his support, and that made it impossible for him to be lenient towards heresy or heretics: for both Convocation and the Commons sought consent for legislation which would strike fear into the heart of the Lollard. As a result, the ugly Act, De Haeretico Comburendo, came into force in 1401. It was to be used with relentless severity against the Lollards and to usher in an age of persecution which would only reach its climax in the fires of Smithfield.

Wycliffe's earliest disciples had not been called upon to stand up for their faith with the courage of those early martyrs who had gone to their death with 'joyful defiance'.[42] Nevertheless two weeks before the new Act came into operation, the first victim of the King's harsh repressive policy went to the stake. This was William Sawtrey, and it fell to him to show the Lollards the way to die. He had been the priest of St. Margaret's Lynn in Norfolk, and then Chaplain of St, Osyth, Walbrook; but in 1400, he found himself arraigned before Convocation on a number of counts. The more significant were that he had said that it was not lawful to adore the cross, but only Christ; that it were better to omit matins and vespers rather than the preaching of God's Word; and, above all, that after Consecration bread in its true nature remained as it was before. He was condemned and burnt to death in the cattle market at Smithfield. No doubt the cruel death of Sawtrey and the still more cruel Act to which it led played their part in Purvey's recantation. He could not find within himself the strength to brave such an ordeal. Was there another element as well? Did he dread to appear in the presence of God as a convicted heretic? That dread was to persist in the case of many others throughout the whole Reformation story.

The records of prosecution during the next few years were all to end with a recantation, and it was not until 1410 that John Badby dared to tread in Sawtrey's footsteps. He was one of the west country Lollards, a tailor or blacksmith from the town of Evesham. He was first brought before the Diocesan court at Worcester and was condemned because he held that the Host was in no sense the body of Christ; it was, he said, inanimate and less worthy of honour or worship than the meanest thing that had life. He was then brought up to London and placed on trial in the presence of 'the whole majesty of Church and State'.[43] But two Archbishops and eight Bishops, the Duke of York and the Chancellor of England, were not enough to overawe him. He would not retract his view that 'Christ, sitting at supper, could not give His disciples His living body to eat'.[44] As a result, he was sentenced to death and a stake was set up in the Smithfield market. The Prince who as Henry V was to win that famous victory at Agincourt stood by while the faggots were piled up round his feet.

The Prince tried long and earnestly to persuade him to recant, promising him life and money if only he would submit. It was all in vain and at last the fire was lit. A humble artisan may have been less sensitive than a highly educated scholar like John Purvey. He knew what he believed and was willing to die for the honour of Christ as the only Saviour. But the pain and torment of the fire made him twist and writhe in a way that led the Prince to see it as a signal of submission. Henry ordered men to pull the faggots away so that he could renew his persuasion and promises. It was to no avail. The fire was re-kindled, and Badby soon succumbed. But, as Trevelyan justly observed, here was something beyond Henry's understanding; 'something before which kings and bishops would one day learn to bow'.[45] Wycliffe and Purvey lived out their days

under the shadow of persecution; Sawtrey and Badby paid
the supreme forfeit as the first two Lollard martyrs. They
were cruelly put to death, but the honour of Christ was
safe in their keeping. Their names deserve to be held in
remembrance to the end of time, for they belong to that
great company who have overcome by the blood of the
Lamb and by the word of their testimony, and who laid
down their lives for Christ and the Gospel.

Perhaps the most remarkable aspect of the Lollard movement was its impact on the Church in Central Europe.
This came about as an unexpected result of the marriage
between Richard II and Anne of Bohemia in January 1382.
Anne was known to have read the Gospels in Latin, Czech,
and German before she came to England, and she may
have had a favourable feeling for the early Lollards. At
some point of time soon after 1390 she was given a copy
of the Lollard work known as 'the doctors on the Gospels'.
This was Purvey's glossed work on the Gospels, consisting
of an exact translation of comments by Jerome, Ambrose,
Augustine, Chrysostom, and many others. Anne sent it to
Archbishop Arundel for his approbation; this was readily
accorded. But she died in 1394 to the great sorrow of king
and people. Archbishop Arundel was to declare: 'It was
more joy of her than of any woman that he ever knew,
for notwithstanding that she was an alien born, she had
in English all the four gospellers, with the doctors upon
them.[46]

During Anne's twelve years in England, Bohemian
courtiers and diplomats travelled freely between Prague
and London, and they took home with them copies of John
Wycliffe's writings. As a result, Wycliffe's vision was soon
diffused in the University of Prague and in the village

communities of Bohemia. His works soon came into the hands of John Huss, and the Hussite movement was the direct product of his teaching. Huss was to translate what Wycliffe had written and to incorporate the text almost verbatim in his own works. When at length the Council of Constance met in 1415, Huss was accused by his enemies of being a Wycliffite, and Wycliffe was denounced as an arch heretic. Huss avowed his admiration for Wycliffe, was condemned, and in spite of the pledge of safe conduct, was burnt at the stake. But the early Moravian Church looked back to Wycliffe through Huss as its spiritual founder and, to this day, there are more manuscript works of Wycliffe in Prague and Vienna than in England.

The true value of the Wycliffite legacy may be judged by the strength of the Lollard movement until it was absorbed by the greater kindred movement of the English Reformation. Persecution was to drive the Lollards off the stage of national attention, but the Act De Haeretico Comburendo did not destroy their underground survival and vigorous influence. Their meetings under cover of darkness were held so that they could read the Lollard Bible or could discuss the tract known as *Wycliffe's Wicket*. This was not from his pen though it bore his name; it was an outspoken and popular attack on the doctrine of transubstantiation. Their love for the Bible in the mother tongue of their own country taught them to feed their souls and to strengthen their faith through its teaching. It was the bridge between Wycliffe and the Reformation.

Modern historians differ on the question as to how far Lollard teaching may have contributed to the insight of the Reformation in matters of doctrine. Persecution had deprived the Lollards in the main of their books, and their teaching had to be passed on by word of mouth. This may explain why the records of the Lollard trials show that the Lollards often differed among themselves on points of faith. But the truth to which they clung was to live on to the dawn of the Reformation. William Tyndale was to publish two old Lollard tracts in order to prove that his theology was not some new-fangled kind of teaching as his opponents insisted. Cranmer was to declare that Wycliffe had proclaimed the truth of the Gospel; Ridley was to comment on the fact that Wycliffe had denied the doctrine of transubstantiation. Hooper was to recall how Wycliffe had opposed the doctrine of the Mass; and Bale was to remark on the fact that Wycliffe had denounced the Friars. Perhaps it was less in formal doctrine than in religious attitude that the Lollards were the authentic precursors of the Reformation. This would explain why so many Lollards who came into contact with the 'Lutheran heresy' at the outset of the Reformation were won by its teaching. The work of John Wycliffe and the witness of the Lollards had made England like a field both plowed and prepared for the good seed of the Reformation. 'The societies of poor men...suddenly finding Europe convulsed by their ideas, seeing their beliefs adopted by the learned and the powerful, joyfully surrendered themselves to the great new movement for which they had been waiting in the dark years so faithfully and so long.'[47]

For Further Reading

G.M. Trevelyan: *England in the Age of Wycliffe*, 1889.

Margaret Beansley: *The Lollard Bible*, 1920.

3

Thomas Bilney
and
the White Horse Inn

The key to an understanding of the English Reformation is rooted and grounded in the Bible. This was firmly summed up in the words of the Sixth of the Thirty Nine Articles which ought never to be overlooked: 'Holy Scripture containeth all things necessary to salvation: so that whatsoever is not read therein, nor may be proved thereby, is not to be required of any man, that it should be believed as an article of faith, or be thought requisite or necessary to salvation.' Not Catholic tradition; not human philosophy; just the revelation of truth in the pages of the Bible. This was why the work of William Tyndale in the translation of the New Testament from Greek into ordinary spoken English was so epoch making. Housewives sitting in the sun, children playing in the street, farmers, scholars, men of all ranks, in all walks of life, could hear the Word of God in language they could understand. And the Bible itself illustrated what this meant in human experience through the life and testimony of so many devoted believers. It was exemplified above all in the Letter in which St Paul drew the veil aside to lay bare his own soul. 'This is a faithful saying and worthy of all acceptance that Christ Jesus came into the world to save sinners, of whom I am chief.' And through Thomas Bilney this would become the key to the English Reformation.

Fifteen hundred years were to pass: then Paul's testimony in this text came to life in the heart of a shy young scholar who had come from Norfolk to study law at Trinity Hall in Cambridge. This was Thomas Bilney, better known as Little Bilney, humble, devout, earnest—in dead earnest about his soul. He had long felt in a vague and indefinite way the emptiness of the religion in which he had been born and bred. His soul was sick and he longed for healing, but he knew not where to find it. He went to the priests, but they could only send him to broken cisterns; they held no water and only mocked his thirst. He knelt at the feet of ignorant confessors and told out all his sins; but they could do no more than prescribe a multitude of penances which wrought no absolution. There were fastings; there were vigils; perhaps payment for masses, perhaps purchase of pardons. He had done all that was required, but for all his fasts and vigils, masses and pardons, he was even worse rather than better. They had brought no consolation and he could only lament: 'There was but small force of strength left in me, who of nature was but weak, small store of money, and very little wit or understanding.[48] He had reached rock bottom, but he would not give up. From time to time a doubt would cross his mind and he wondered if there were any real value in the mumbo-jumbo of those mediaeval exercises. Had they brought him closer to God? Had they pointed him to Jesus in Whom all the treasures of forgiveness and acceptance are found? This was more than Bilney could yet perceive...he had found no comfort and was neither eased nor relieved in his secret distress. He was still weighed down by the heavy burden of sin that threatened to crush his soul. But dark as was the night; dawn was at hand.

'At last,' Bilney was to affirm, 'I heard speak of Jesus, even then, when the New Testament was first set forth by Erasmus'.[49] It was in March 1516 that Erasmus brought out his first edition of the Greek text of the New Testament. It was entitled the *Novum Instrumentum*; the Greek text was in one column and a fresh Latin translation by Erasmus in the other. There was a formal prohibition against any attempt to bring copies into the precincts of Cambridge whether 'by horse or by boat or on wheels or on foot'.[50] But in 1519 Erasmus brought out a second edition entitled the *Novum Testamentum* and the Greek text was of enormous consequence. But men were also full of praise for the Latin translation in the parallel column and Bilney bought a copy mainly for the sake of the Latin version. But the finger of God was at work; it was as though a light from heaven began to shine within his soul. 'And at the first time of reading, as I well remember', so he wrote, 'I chanced upon this sentence of St Paul (O most sweet and comfortable sentence to my soul!), "It is a true saying, and worthy of all men to be embraced, that Christ Jesus came into the world to save sinners of whom I am the chief."'[51] The original in Latin was strikingly emphatic:

'*O mihI suavissimam PaulI sententiam*'.[52] Those words of
St Paul seemed to stand out in letters of light and that
luminous quality was enough to scatter all his lingering
unbelief. It would serve no purpose for Bilney to dispute
with Paul as to who was the chief of sinners: enough to
know that Christ had come to save men just like him.
Bilney could not tell just what had happened, but one
thing he did know. Whereas he was bruised and on the
edge of despair, now his heart overflowed with joy. 'This
one sentence', he wrote, 'through God's instruction and
inward working, which I did not then perceive, did so
exhilarate my heart...that immediately I felt a marvellous
comfort and quietness'.[53]

Bilney could not keep the joy of that discovery to
himself; he had to tell others. 'There was never a more
innocent and upright man in all England', so Foxe
declared,[54] and his guileless sincerity soon began to attract
his friends to share his new found faith. He was perhaps
the first Cambridge scholar to provide an impulse that led
to the movement for the English Reformation, and that
movement had its cradle among his friends who used to
meet night by night at the White Horse Inn. This was just
across the street from *Corpus ChristI* where it stood on
a block of land which belonged to St Catherine's. There
was a small postern door which opened on to Milne
Street, or Queens' Lane as it is today, and this allowed
men to come and go without undue notice. Bilney was
the leading spirit among these men who used to thread
their way down Milne Street in the dusk of evening. Their
numbers would fluctuate with the passage of time, but
a roll-call of their names is truly impressive. There were
Thomas Arthur and John Thixtill, Robert Barnes and

George Stafford, Matthew Parker and John Lambert, John Rogers and Miles Coverdale. There were Doctors, Fellows, Masters, Scholars, all intent on one thing. They came to pore over the text of the *Novum Testamentum*, and so doing, to find strength and encouragement in each other's company. Bilney was the central figure in that band of friends, and the recovered loveliness of personal devotion and Christian fellowship was their strength and shield. It was the glad morning of the Reformation, still too early to see the dark shadows that were to fall. What the White Horse Inn meant to them was well summed up in the words of Thomas Becon: 'So oft as I was in their company,' he wrote long afterwards, 'methought I was quietly placed in the new glorious Jerusalem.'[55]

Little Bilney had an almost naïve belief that others would respond to the gospel as he had done if they only heard his testimony. He told out all his heart both to Cuthbert Tunstall and to Cardinal Wolsey; in vain. It would prove otherwise in the case of Hugh Latimer who in 1522 became one of twelve men licensed to preach throughout the realm. Then in 1523 George Stafford entered on a course of lectures to large crowds of eager students on the text of Holy Scripture. This provoked Latimer beyond sufferance, perhaps all the more so because his own mind was ill at ease. It was still the custom for those who had taken a degree in Divinity as he did in 1524 to deliver an Oration on some aspect of their studies. Latimer determined, with the zeal of violent prejudice at the spread of Reformed doctrine, to take up the cudgels at the highest level. He left Stafford for a far more illustrious adversary and set out to castigate Philip Melancthon who had lately impugned the School Doctors. He had been dismayed to see how many students had left off the study of the Schoolmen for the reading of the Scriptures. What was 'this new-fangled kind of study'?[56] Where were the old text books which had always been in use before they had turned to Greek and Hebrew? Latimer was eloquent as always, but intemperate; too strong indeed to ring quite true. Perhaps there was something in the preacher's manner, perhaps in the tone of certain remarks: enough to show that this was zeal without knowledge, zeal that knew no peace or comfort within. But there was one hidden in that crowd of hearers, perhaps because of his diminutive stature, one to whom the secret disharmony in the preacher's soul was clear as daylight. This was Thomas Bilney: but who was he, and what could he do?

Bilney saw at once that he stood in the presence of a man who was caught in the same kind of web as that in which his own soul had long been entangled. Foxe said that he was 'stricken with a brotherly pity towards him, and bethought by what means he might best win this zealous, ignorant brother to the true knowledge of Christ.'[57] His heart went out to him as one who was still in error in spite of his rugged honesty and homely eloquence. He was only Little Bilney and would never do any great thing for God; but let God give him the soul of that man, and what great things would he do in His Name! Therefore after a short delay he sought Latimer in the vestry of St Edward's Church and begged him for the love of God to hear his confession. Here was Bilney with his shy and guileless sincerity asking the great preacher to shrive his soul! What could it mean? Latimer did not understand all at once, but he would never forget that day. 'Bilney...desired me for God's sake to hear his confession,' so he recalled many years later in a sermon before the Duchess of Suffolk. 'I did so, and to say the truth, by his confession I learned more than before in many years.'[58] Latimer thought that he was to hear a confession of sin and was prepared to listen with patience. But there can be no doubt as to the tenor of that confession. Bilney told him with touching simplicity his own story of conflict and anguish, and how he had found comfort and relief at last when he turned to the *Novum Testamentum*. Perhaps he drew that little book out of his pocket and let it fall open at the words of St Paul. And Latimer would hear him read that 'most sweet and comfortable word': 'It is a true saying, and worthy of all men to be embraced, that Christ Jesus came into the world to save sinners, of whom I am chief.'

The great preacher had been taken by storm. He had heard the voice of God as well as the voice of Bilney, and he could not resist the truth. That quiet story of a long and painful conflict, and that testimony to the pardon and peace of God, told out in the solemn stillness of that vestry, awoke in his heart new thoughts and feelings too deep for words. Bilney had brought him an insight into the grace of God such as he had never known before. It was like a Divine Secret which had now been revealed in all its wonder and love. The result was immediate. It was not the penitent confessor to whom the Word of God came in absolution that day; it was the great preacher who came on the bended knees of his soul to find pardon and peace with God. Perhaps one of his first acts would be to procure for himself a copy of that little book he had so despised; it was to hang from his girdle to the day of his death. He would often recall what had taken place in that quiet vestry and could never speak of Bilney without an accent of divine animation. 'Master Bilney, or rather Saint Bilney,...was the instrument whereby God called me to knowledge, for I may thank him, next to God, for that knowledge that I have in the Word of God.'[59] He forsook his studies in the Schoolmen and joined Bilney's ring of friends in the White Horse Inn. He sought out George Stafford to ask his pardon for the rude attack he had made the year before. Latimer and Bilney became inseparable, and this was 'much noted of many' in Cambridge.[60] They used to walk almost daily in the fields round Cambridge; they went together on errands of mercy to those who were poor or in prison. And their hearts would burn within them as Jesus Himself drew near and went with them.

There was yet one other whose name can not be overlooked; this was Thomas Cranmer. As a Fellow of Jesus College in the 1520s, he could hardly have been ignorant of the ferment which was growing up round Bilney and Latimer, but he does not appear to have been in contact with them. He pursued his study of the Scriptures with the clear recognition of their supreme authority, but new ideas only won their way into his mind by slow and painful footsteps. His name was not linked with the White Horse Inn, but Bilney's testimony had become widely known in Cambridge circles. Then in 1535 he was suddenly appointed Archbishop of Canterbury; he was far too cautious to commit himself without reserve to new Reformed doctrines while Henry VIII was on the throne. His great achievement during those years was the publication of what became known as the Great Bible with the King's licence in 1537. Cranmer could not conceal his joy; it was more to his liking 'than any other translation heretofore made'.[61] After the royal sanction had been obtained, he wrote to Cromwell: 'My Lord, for this your pain taken in this behalf, I give unto you my most hearty thanks, assuring Your Lordship…you have shewed me more pleasure than if you had given me a thousand pound: and I doubt not that hereby such fruit of good knowledge shall ensue that it shall well appear hereafter what high and acceptable service you have done.'[62] Henry died in 1547 with his hand held fast by Cranmer: 'no last rite …, no extreme unction, just an evangelical statement of faith in the grip of (that) hand.'[63] The accession of Edward VI liberated Cranmer from so many inhibitions and his faith was at last free to burst into full blossom. Nowhere was this more apparent than in the *Book of Common Prayer* issued in 1549 and enforced by an Act of Uniformity, followed by a revised edition and a second Act in 1552. At the heart of each Book lay the Service of the Holy Communion.

Cranmer did not arrive at a fully reformed doctrine of the Lord's Supper until fairly late in life. He had long since ceased to believe that the Mass was a sacrifice of the body and blood, soul and divinity, of Christ for the sins of the living and of the dead. But he passed through more than one phase before he reached his own *ne plus ultra*. Was there a Lutheran phase? Was the presence of Christ attached in some way to the bread and wine? Was there a Zwinglian phase? Did he think of the bread and wine as mere signs or symbols? What he came to believe was that Christ is present in the hearts of His faithful people: they take the bread and drink the wine to feed on Him by faith with thanksgiving. And embodied in the heart of the 1552 Service for the Lord's Supper were four 'comfortable words' from the New Testament. The first two were chosen from the Gospels and introduced by the dignified formula: 'Hear what comfortable words our Saviour Christ saith unto all that truly turn to him.' The choice was predictable: 'Come unto me all that travail and are heavy laden, and I will refresh you' (Mt. 11:2); 'So God loved the world, that he gave his only begotten Son, to the end that all who believe in him should not perish, but have everlasting life' (Jn. 3:16). The third verse was taken from a Pauline Letter. If the choice had been left to a modern Liturgiologist, there might well have been some hesitation. How could he choose just one word from Letters that were studded with so many priceless sayings, and what word would that be? Cranmer had no hesitation. He knew the one verse which had a unique place in the story of the English Reformation. 'Hear also what Saint Paul saith', he wrote, 'This is a true saying, and worthy of all men to be received, that Christ Jesus came into the world to save sinners' (1 Tim. 1:15). That was the heart of the gospel. He came; He came to save; He came to save sinners. And Paul's testimony had rung down the ages to sound in the ears of Little Bilney; then through Cranmer it found its way into the *Book of Common Prayer*, and thence into the life and soul of many generations.

It was about the year 67 AD that St Paul was led out through the gate of the Imperial City to die by the sword in the hand of a Roman soldier. He had long had a martyr's heart; at last he faced a martyr's death; and he had won a martyr's crown. But his text and testimony were to shine through the Dark Ages and flame with light once more in the English Reformation. Bilney was to die in the Lollards' pit at Norwich in 1531; Latimer would be bound back to back with Ridley and burnt at the stake in 1555. Cranmer would die with a heroic confidence just outside the walls of Oxford in 1556. Each in turn was to pass through that ordeal with a courage that was beyond all praise. But the funeral pyre in Norwich or Oxford could only touch what was mortal. Beyond the pains and pangs of death there was a far graver issue. They had been condemned as heretics, and an impenitent heretic was consigned to the flames of hell. What if they had made a mistake? What if the Church were right and they were wrong? The fires in Norwich and Oxford were as nothing to the fires in hell. Bilney and Latimer and Cranmer were no stronger in themselves than other men are, but they did not flinch at the stake. Their real greatness was the courage which held them fast in the hour of death. They overcame by the blood of the Lamb, and they loved not their lives unto death. That 'faithful saying ' of St Paul, that 'sweet and comfortable word' of Little Bilney, helped them to lift their eyes from earth to heaven and to endure as those who saw Jesus at the right hand of God: none other than Jesus, Who 'came into the world to save sinners'. There would be no room for argument as to who was the chief; they could only kneel in spirit on the sacred ground of Calvary. And when they sang, it would be a new song. 'Worthy art thou, O Lord, for thou wast slain, and didst purchase unto God with thy blood, men of every tribe and tongue' (Rev. 5:9 RV).

For Further Reading

Stephen Cattley: *The Acts and Monuments of John Foxe* (8 vols.), 1841.

Hugh Latimer: *Works* (Two Volumes), Parker Society, 1844-45.

J.J. Batley: *On a Reformer's Bible, being an Essay on the Adversaries in the Vulgate of Thomas Bilney,* 1940.

Frederic Seebohm: *The Oxford Reformers,* 1911.

Harold S. Darby: *Hugh Latimer* (Epworth Press), 1953.

Thomas Cranmer: *Works* (Two Volumes), Parker Society, 1844-46.

A.F. Pollard: *Thomas Cranmer and The English Reformation* (new edition), 1926.

Diarmaid McCulloch, *Thomas Cranmer,* 1995.

4

George Whitefield
and
the Everlasting Gospel

Far the greatest movement for God among English people since the Reformation was the spiritual awakening under Whitefield and the Wesleys in the eighteenth century. George Whitefield had enrolled as a servitor at Pembroke College in the Michaelmas term of 1732. Oxford had perhaps never sunk to so low an ebb of academic thought or spiritual life as at that time. There were few lectures and still less learning. The chief centres of social activity were the cock-pit and the tavern. Gentlemen commoners in powdered wigs lounged in Lyne's Coffee House or made love to tradesmen's daughters in Merton Walks. But George Whitefield was an earnest seeker for God and strove to live up to such light as he had. It was to Charles Wesley that he came to owe his first all-important

Christian contact. Some time before, Charles had gathered round him a small group of serious-minded young men. Then his bother John returned to Oxford and took up his duties as a Fellow of Lincoln. He soon took his place at the head of Charles and his friends, and they began to meet in his rooms each evening in order to study the Greek text of the New Testament.

But they went much further than this. They passed under review what each had done during the day and planned what steps each should take on the morrow. They took the Sacrament once a month and addressed themselves to care for the sick and the poor. They began to visit the gaol to read and pray with those who were in prison and they set up a school in the slums, paying the mistress and clothing the children. They were laughed at as Bible Moths or mocked as the Holy Club. Many other names were coined, but the name that stuck was the word Methodist. Whitefield soon stood in the forefront of that little circle. He seems to have felt a particular longing to cultivate the humility of Christ. This led him to practise the most rigorous forms of austerity. It was as though personal holiness could be obtained as a reward for self-denial and self-discipline. At length he shut himself up for six weeks in his study and made himself seriously ill. Charles Wesley sought him out and took him to see John who advised him to resume all known duties, but to rely on none for inward peace and holiness. Change was at hand. The year 1735 saw the dispersion of the Methodists far and wide. The Wesleys left England in October for their short-lived ministry in the colony of Georgia. Not long before, George Whitefield had been born again.

Whitefield was the first in that band of friends to get a firm understanding of the gospel. He was to say that the turning point came when Charles Wesley lent him a book by Henry Scougall called *The Life of God in the Soul of Man*. He saw for the first time that a man must be born again or perish. He took that book in his hand and began to pray that if he were not yet born again, God would bring it to pass. He read on to learn that true religion consists in a vital union of the soul with God; that is, Christ must be formed within the heart by faith. This was not long before Easter 1737 and it shone like a ray from the sun in his soul. He began to write letters to all his kith and kin, and to speak to fellow students, telling them that there was such a thing as the new birth until they thought that he was off his head. But he was not off his head; he had grasped the secret of everlasting life. It did not lie in tears for sin nor zeal for God; it could be found only in Christ through faith. 'It may be superstitious perhaps,' he once confessed, 'but whenever I go to Oxford, I can not help running to that place where Jesus Christ first revealed Himself to me and gave me the new birth.'[64]

In June 1735, after nine terms at Oxford, he undertook a visit to his family in Gloucester. He was soon made instrumental in the awakening of souls to the reality of things unseen and he formed a little band of brethren on the model of the group at Oxford. He began to read the Bible on his knees, trying to pray line by line over what he had just read. When he returned to Oxford in March 1736, his heart was full of the pains and pleasures of the new birth. He had won the favourable regard of Bishop Benson of Gloucester who offered to ordain him as soon as he was ready. He was only twenty one when on Trinity Sunday in

June 1736 he was made a Deacon in Gloucester Cathedral. 'I could think of nothing,' he wrote, 'but Samuel's standing, a little child before the Lord.'[65] He preached his first sermon the next Sunday to a crowded congregation in St Mary the Crypt, and a complaint was at once lodged with the Bishop to the effect that he had driven fifteen people out of their wits. The good Bishop merely expressed the hope that their madness would not be forgotten before the next Sunday.

Whitefield's career as a preacher and evangelist had begun. During 1537, churches in Bristol and London were packed to the point of suffocation when it was known that he would preach. Thousands who came ready to scoff were taken by storm. Weekdays found him at Ludgate and/or Newgate, and in many other churches as well. Sundays began at six in the morning at Forster Lane or Cripplegate, and he went on to preach three or four more times in the course of the day. All this involved having to walk ten or twelve miles as he made his way from church to church. Before daylight on each Sunday morning, the streets would be alive with men, lanterns in hand, as they hurried to get a seat in the church where he was to preach: thousands were turned away for want of room. But this was to cause great umbrage among clergy whose churches were emptied. As a result, in 1739, he found that one by one every church in London and Bristol was closed to him. He was at last driven to take a step which set the course for the rest of his life. He turned away from church pulpits where he was no longer welcome, and took to the open air as a field preacher.

Whitefield's thoughts turned to the Kingswood Colliers just beyond Bristol where they lived in a state of desperate need and poverty. After much prayer, he walked out to Hannam Mount on Saturday afternoon February 17th 1739 and preached to a small crowd of some two hundred colliers. The news soon spread, and though it was in the depth of winter, the crowd grew in number each time he returned. The two hundred on February 17th had swollen to ten thousand by February 25th, and that ten thousand to more than twenty thousand by March 18th. The fields and lanes were thick with men whose cheeks were as black as the pits in which they toiled and their tell-tale response could be gauged in the white furrows caused by the tears which ran down their blackened faces. Whitefield may have been forced out of church and pulpit, but he had found the true field for his labours. Back in London he began to preach every Sunday at Moorefields in the morning and at Kennington Common in the evening. Weekdays found him at places like Hackney and Mayfair, Smithfield and Blackheath. The crowd often numbered more than twenty thousand, and his voice could sometimes be heard a mile away. Thousands came who would never have heard a sermon inside a church, but they listened as for eternity when he preached in the open air. The die had thus been cast: he was to become an itinerant evangelist without precedent and without equal in the British Isles and the American colonies.

Seven times in all Whitefield was to cross the Atlantic in order to visit the New World in America, and his ministry as it unfolded was almost equally divided between Britain and the colonies. His first voyage landed him at Savannah in Georgia in May 1738, but it was a whirlwind visit which led him to return after only four months in order to obtain Priest's Orders. In August 1739 he sailed once more for

America and soon embarked on a long preaching tour that took him from Savannah to Philadelphia, thence to New York, and on to Boston where he preached to thousands on the famous Common. It was in New England that he was always thenceforth assured of a tumultuous welcome and the effect of his preaching was perhaps even more astonishing than at home in Britain. His contact with Benjamin Franklin in Philadelphia was highly significant; his meeting with Jonathan Edwards in Northampton even more so. It was through his powerful ministry that the fire was kindled which broke out in genuine revival throughout the New World in the forties. One of the last sermons he was ever to preach rang out with the same clear invitation: 'Though the sun is going down, though the shadow of the evening is coming on, God is willing, O man, …to be a sinner's God: He has found a way whereby He can be reconciled to you.'[66]

Whitefield owed a great deal to John and Charles Wesley when he first went up to Oxford and the bond of friendship between all three was to endure to the end of their lives. But it is my deliberate judgment that the Wesleys owed the greater debt to Whitefield. He was 'a man in Christ' for twelve months before the two Wesleys found peace with God. It was Whitefield who had constrained John to engage in field preaching: and the message they proclaimed with glorious certainty was the same old-fashioned gospel which had seldom been heard since the last days of the Puritan veterans. It might be said that their preaching was experimental rather than evangelical, but it was based on sound theology, and the discovery that what they preached was the doctrine of the Reformers and the Articles gave them solid reassurance.

Their great desire was to uplift the Lord Jesus as the only Saviour and to call men with urgency and compassion to come to God through faith in Him.

With the passage of time, certain divergences were to arise and to cause a painful rift between Whitefield and the Wesleys. Whitefield was a moderate Calvinist; Wesley an avowed Arminian: and this drove a wedge between them that was never completely overcome. But in September 1747 Whitefield wrote a healing letter. 'As for universal redemption,' he told Wesley, 'if we omit on each side the talking for or against reprobation, which we may do fairly, and agree as we already do in giving a universal offer to all poor sinners that will come and take of the water of life, I think we may manage very well.'[67] But there was a further breach with Whitefield over Wesley's doctrine of Christian Perfection. Yet not even Wesley could have asked for more than Whitefield felt that he could humbly claim for himself. 'Thanks be to His great Name,' he declared in 1753, 'I can truly say that for these many years past, no sin hath had dominion over me, neither have I slept with the guilt of any known, unrepented sin upon my heart.'[68]

Whitefield travelled the length and breadth of the British Isles and the American colonies for thirty years. He would preach twice or thrice on the Sunday and several times during the week; each sermon might be an hour in length, and it seemed as though he never preached without effect. Henry Venn could only marvel that he could use his voice for some fifty hours a week to address many thousands, and do so week after week, year in and year out, and then remain up to midnight in prayer and praise with his friends and hosts.[69] Only eighty one of his sermons were to appear in print; of these seventy five were published in

a single volume. The first forty five were in print before
he was twenty five years old, and the last eighteen were
taken down in shorthand and published without any kind
of revision or correction. Ryle said that his scribes were
equally ignorant of grammar and the gospel.[70] Whitefield
himself cried out in pain when he read their loose
and inaccurate reports. Yet with all their faults, these
sermons repay a close reading and throw some light on
the technique of his preaching. His diction was faultless,
plain and lucid to a degree; no one could fail to grasp its
meaning, whether or not they liked it. He seldom vexed
his hearers with reasons that were involved or abstruse; he
saw his mark and shot at it with direct and unerring aim.
Simple statements of truth and apt illustrations were part
of the fabric of his preaching, but they only came to life
with power and passion when uttered aloud by Whitefield.
His flashing eyes and trembling lips, his silent weeping and
thrilling appeals, were signs that no one could mistake.
'If any one were to ask me who was the second preacher
I ever heard, I should be at some loss to answer,' said good
old John Newton; 'but in regard to the first, Mr Whitefield
exceeded so far every other man of my time that I should
be at none.'[71]

It was as a preacher of the everlasting gospel that
George Whitefield's name will always be held in honoured
remembrance. He was far the greatest evangelist English
speaking people have ever known. He was endowed
with a voice of exceptional strength and beauty and he
managed it with perfect control in order to reflect every
emotion. It was like a deep and well-tuned organ and he
could sweep every chord of human feeling. He knew how
to pitch his voice so that it would carry to the edge of the

largest crowd, and its carrying properties have rarely been excelled. Plymouth people used to say that he was often distinctly heard at the distance of a full mile across the stretch of water between Tor Point and the New Passage. Tradition says that when he preached at Bristol, his voice was heard over a mile away on Staincliffe Hill as he cried 'O earth, earth, earth, hear the Word of the Lord!' Benjamin Franklin declared as the result of an experiment that he could be heard in the open air without effort by a crowd of thirty thousand. And all this in an age when there were no artificial aids or public address systems to help with sound. The range and strength of his voice were phenomenal and were enhanced by the singing of Wesley's hymns. The sheer volume of Charles Wesley's output leaves no surprise that so much of it was ephemeral. What does surprise is the fact that so much of what he wrote has never been excelled and his genius was seen in the combination of poetry and metaphor with dignity and devotion at the deepest levels of thought and worship. Whitefield wrote no hymns, but he loved to quote them and to hear them sung. What must it have been like to have thirty thousand men and women pour out their hearts as they sang: 'Lo, He comes with clouds descending, Once for favoured sinners slain!'

Whitefield's oratory was suffused with dramatic qualities which were more than enough to sweep his hearers off their feet. He could describe a scene or tell a story by way of illustration in such vivid terms that it seemed to live before men's eyes. There was his great picture of a ship in a storm at sea, with masts gone and hull down; it came to a thrilling climax as his voice rang out with a cry as though he did not know what next to do. But the sailors in the crowd knew, and they thundered as one man in reply: 'The long-boat! Man the long-boat!'[72] But the sailors were unlearned and ignorant men: how would the Lords and Ladies of the upper class in society respond? In 1748 the Countess of Huntingdon appointed him as one of her chaplains and made her home at Chelsea available for him to preach 'privately to them which were of reputation' (Gal. 2:2). These small but brilliant assemblies met week by week and brought together people like Chesterfield and Bolingbroke who heard him with rapt attention. They heard the most famous illustration of all when he described a blind man skirting the edge of a precipice, decrepit with age and deserted by his dog: his staff was seen to slip through his nerveless fingers and he stooped to retrieve it, bending all unaware over the cliff and then stumbling forward. Lord Chesterfield was electrified; he sprang from his seat with the startled cry 'Good God! He's gone!'[73] No one could sleep through a sermon like that; it was far too urgent to be ignored. Illustrations of that kind might have been dismissed as too melodramatic on the lips of a lesser man, but they never palled when backed by Whitefield's tremendous earnestness. The more he preached, the more did it whet the edge of desire for men to hear, and hear again. And God used him to rouse Britain and New England from the sleep of death to light and life immortal.

In September 1769 Whitefield embarked on his seventh and final visit to America, and soon began to preach almost daily in his old style. He settled his affairs in Savannah, spent the month of May 1770 in Philadelphia, and then went on to New England for his last tour. He fell seriously ill in September, but went on preaching until the morning of September 29th. He was persuaded to preach at a place called Exeter; it was to prove his last sermon. He stood for some minutes before he found his voice, but then began in a strain of rapture. 'Works! Works!' he cried, in a voice like thunder, 'A man get to heaven by works? I would as soon think of climbing to the moon on a rope of sand.'[74] He then rode on to spend the night with friends at Newbury Port. The house in which he stayed is still standing, though now divided by a partition down the central stairway so as to form two homes. Whitefield supped with his hosts and then bade them good night in order to retire early. But as he climbed the stairs, candle in hand, he could not resist the desire to turn round and speak once more. And as he spoke, the fire kindled, and he did not stop until the light of the candle had burnt down and gone out in its socket.[75] Then at last he withdrew to his bedroom where a violent attack of spasmodic asthma seized him. He fought for breath between intervals of broken sleep until soon after four o'clock in the morning. A fresh fit of coughing woke him up and he knew that death was not far away. But he went on fighting for breath by the open window until the day began to break. At six o'clock on that morning, September 30th 1770, he fetched a gasp and breathed no more. At the age of fifty five, the prince of English preachers was dead; a prince without a peer. 'Let the name of Whitefield perish,' he cried, 'if only Christ be magnified.'

For Further Reading

Works by George Whitefield:
   Vol. I Letters I to CCCXCVII.
   Vol. II Letters LCCXVIII to DCCCCLXIV

Vol. III Letters DCCCCLXV to MCCCCLXV.
Vol. IV Tracts and Other Writings
Vol. V Sermons I to XXXI.
Vol. VI Sermons XXXII to LIX.

Other Works:

John Gillies: *The Life of the Rev. George Whitefield* (New Edition, 1838).

L. Tyerman: *The Life of the Rev. George Whitefield* (Second Edition, 1890).

J.C. Ryle: *Christian Leaders of the Last Century* (New Edition 1880).

A Member of the Houses of Shirley and Hastings: *The Life and Times of Selina, Countess of Huntingdon* (1839).

James Stephen: *Essays in Ecclesiastical Biography* (New Edition 1875).

G.R. Balleine: *A History of The Evangelical Party* (New Edition 1933).

M.L. Loane: *Oxford and The Evangelical Succession* (Christian Focus Publications, 2006).

5

William Wilberforce
and
Evangelical Continuity

Far the greatest movement for God among English people since the Reformation was the spiritual awakening in the eighteenth century. The great heralds of that movement were George Whitefield and the Wesleys. They were itinerant evangelists who from the mid-thirties onwards gave their lives to travel the length and breadth of the British Isles and the American Colonies in order to proclaim the glad tidings of God's love for sinful men and women. Their labours, measured by any standard, were nothing less than heroic. No hardship, no opposition, no mob violence, and no social ostracism could make them keep silent. The century in which they lived was known as the Age of Enlightenment, but no age could have sunk into greater spiritual darkness. They had to break through the crust of apathy and ignorance to reach men's hearts, and they did so by their powerful preaching. Church doors were closed to them, but they took to the open air in city and in country alike. Crowds of up to thirty thousand often came to hear them on the coldest winter mornings; thousands went away believing. Nor did Whitefield and the Wesleys stand alone. God raised up men like Walker of Truro, Grimshaw of Haworth, Berridge of Everton, Romaine of London, and Henry Venn of Huddersfield and Yelling; there were many others as well. These men all had a fixed centre for their ministry; they were parochial clergy, though some like Grimshaw and Berridge often crossed parish boundaries to preach elsewhere. Their great concern was for the souls of men, and the gospel they preached came straight from the pages of the Bible. They were always calling for conversion, and assurance, and holiness. Whitefield's mighty preaching, John Wesley's class meetings and lay preachers, and Charles Wesley's hymns went far to change the face of England. Walker died in 1761; Grimshaw in 1763; Whitefield in 1770; but that generation did not come to an end until the closing decade of the century and the death of John Wesley in 1791, and Berridge in 1793, and Romaine in 1795, and Henry Venn in 1797. Their names will always be held in honour; they were the Evangelists of England.

No hard and fast line can be drawn between one generation and another; there will always be elements of overlap and interplay in successive periods. The men who bridged the close of the eighteenth century and the dawn of the nineteenth century may be reckoned as the second generation in the Evangelical movement. Their life and work were cast in a totally different milieu from that in which

Whitefield and the Wesleys had been born and nurtured, and they were more firmly anchored within the norms of the Church of England. Wesley's death led to the formal separation of the Methodists from the Church of their fathers; Henry Venn's influence virtually brought to an end the practice of field preaching beyond parish boundaries; the more moderate disciples of George Whitefield were confirmed and strengthened in church loyalties. Who were these men? There was Thomas Scott, 1747–1821, whose book *The Force of Truth* had traced his spiritual journey from the arid wastes of Arian philosophy to the solid rocks of Christian conviction and whose Commentary on the Bible was to be a vade mecum in godly homes for a hundred years. There was Richard Cecil, 1748–1810, with his fashionable congregation in the Chapel-of-Ease in Bedford Row. There was John Venn, 1759–1813, with his notable ministry as Rector of Clapham. But the foremost leader in that generation was John Newton, 1725–1807, whose life story had been one of truly 'amazing grace'. He could look back from the close of his life to his early friendship with Whitefield and Grimshaw while he was at Liverpool; or his friendship with William Cowper and Mary Unwin while he was at Olney; or his later friendship with Simeon and Wilberforce while he was in London. It was the vision and dedication of Newton, and Scott, and Cecil which had led to the foundation of the Eclectic Society in 1783, and the Church Missionary Society in 1799, and the British and Foreign Bible Society in 1804. The new century found in such men the pioneers of an ever expanding radius of work for the world-wide spread of the everlasting gospel.

The two most influential leaders in the third generation were Charles Simeon, 1759–1836, and William Wilberforce,

1759–1833. They were born in the same year, and they died within three years of each other. Simeon had gone up to Cambridge as a Scholar of King's College in 1779 and had found the secret of forgiveness and acceptance with God in his first term. The most powerful of all incentives for a life of service had gripped his soul and he held on his way thenceforth with a perseverance that was never to flag. He was ordained in May 1782 and in November was appointed as Incumbent of Holy Trinity in the heart of Cambridge. He was thereafter to reside as a Fellow of King's and to preach at Holy Trinity to the close of his life fifty four years later. There were many difficulties at first; they stemmed from town and gown alike; but he stood his ground through thick and thin. Undergraduates were to discover that he was a fearless preacher of truth; they flocked to his church in ever growing numbers. He soon made them welcome to his Sermon Classes and his Conversation Parties, and he sponsored a new style of preaching based on faithful exposition of the text of Scripture. His influence was to reach out to the furthest corners of Church and Realm; his disciples were to provide the real strength of Evangelical continuity in the Victorian era. Through his friendship with Charles Grant, he came to exercise what all knew to be the controlling influence in the choice of Chaplains for the East India Company, and he used it with rare faith and foresight. He was deeply involved in the birth of the Church Missionary Society in 1799 and the Church Mission to the Jews in 1814. He founded the London Clerical Education Society in 1816 and the Simeon Trust in 1819 with the aim of making sure that vacant livings would be filled by godly clergy. 'If you knew what his authority and influence were,' Lord Macaulay was to write, 'and how they extended from

Cambridge to the most remote corners of England, you would allow that his real sway in the Church was far greater than that of any Primate.'[76]

Wilberforce had gone up to St John's College Cambridge in 1776 and had entered the House of Commons in 1780. He was small and slightly deformed, but this was made up for by his sparkling wit and sunny nature. His great friend was William Pitt who at the age of twenty four became Prime Minister in 1783. Wilberforce was to undergo the most radical change in his life as a result of his conversion in November 1785. During the next twelve months he was caught in the tension of one who stood between two worlds, but the die was cast by the end of that year when he agreed to bring the whole question of the slave trade to the bar of the House. He was one of the most gifted orators in that age of mighty orators; neither Burke, nor Fox, nor Pitt excelled him in this respect. Progress in the anti-slave trade campaign was by slow and painful degrees, but in 1792 a vote in the House of Commons made it clear that nothing less than total abolition of this traffic was now in sight. A new factor in his own life emerged that year, one which was to have a permanent influence on his public career: he began to share with Henry Thornton the home at Battersea Rise in Clapham. Later when he married he moved into Broomfield across the lawn between the two houses. Close by were the homes of Charles Grant and James Stephen; and soon there were others. The Rector of Clapham was John Venn who became spiritual guide and mentor to this remarkable group of laymen. Most of them were or soon became members of the House of Commons and their combined talent was the equal to that in Pitt's Cabinet. They were known as the Clapham Sect, and

Wilberforce was their acknowledged leader. They were of one heart and mind in the long struggle to do away with the slave trade, and at last in 1807 the bill for Abolition became law. It was a great triumph for Wilberforce, for the Clapham Sect, for a host of voluntary workers, and above all, for the impact of the gospel on the legislative forces in the Commons. Wilberforce himself could never feel content until slavery itself was abolished, but in 1823 leadership was to pass from him to Thomas Fowell Buxton. Ten years later as he lay on his death bed he was told of the crowning mercy in his life: the Bill of Emancipation had been carried.

There were many godly men in that third generation, though not of the outstanding calibre of Charles Simeon: men like Josiah Pratt, 1768–1844, and Edward Bickersteth, 1786–1850, and Daniel Wilson, 1778–1858. There is clear-cut testimony from all sides as to the strength and far-reaching influence of their life and witness. Canon Liddon, a strong Tractarian, was to observe in his *Life of Pusey*: 'The world to come, with its boundless issues of life and death, the infinite value of the one Atonement, the regenerating, purifying, guiding action of God the Holy Spirit in respect of the Christian soul, were preached to our grandfathers with a force and earnestness which are beyond controversy. The deepest and most fervid religion in England during the first three decades of this century was that of the Evangelicals.'[77] Liddon's observation was a retrospective judgment as he looked back from the latter part of the century; but as early as in 1830, Thomas Arnold, a Broad Churchman, had come from a totally different standpoint to the same view. 'Although Evangelicalism... be not the perfection of Christianity,' he had written, 'yet it is Christianity vital and essential.'[78] But that is only part of the story; there were reverse feelings as well. Subtle undercurrents in the Church as a whole were well at work even before the rise of the Tractarian Movement. This was made clear in the case of Samuel Wilberforce who went up to Oxford in 1823 and soon began to move away from the Conservative background of his childhood. He was careful to avoid all friendships within the Evangelical enclaves of Wadham and St Edmund Hall. 'He had a fear of being thought 'peculiar', and in any case, reported to his father that he found the young men who advertised themselves as religious a dull and vulgar lot.'[79] Many of them, he said, had but 'little notion of the painful process of personal commitment which had endowed the Evangelicalism of an earlier generation with its real substance.'[80]

There can be no doubt that the great impulse from Simeon at Cambridge and Wilberforce at Clapham gave rise to a steady increase in the number of dedicated clergy and godly laymen in the Victorian era; but the Evangelical movement as a whole had ceased to throw up the charismatic leaders of its earlier history. There was no one who could adequately fill the shoes of Simeon or of Wilberforce until Lord Ashley came to the fore. His great sphere of action from 1826 to 1851 was the House of Commons; then he went to the House of Lords as the seventh Earl of Shaftesbury. All that Wilberforce had been as the friend of the slave, Shaftesbury was to become as the friend of the poor. Mill hands, pit boys, chimney sweeps, ragged schools, milliners, dress makers, lodging houses, lunacy asylums: all bespoke his concern in a way that went far beyond the process of legislation. No holds were barred in the struggle to obstruct or oppose his Ten

Hour Bill, but he held on his course with iron tenacity. It took its place at last on the Statute Book in 1847 and the worst of the long entrenched evils were swept away. No assessment of Shaftesbury will ever be valid unless it takes into account the fact that his supreme desire was to be the bearer of the very comfort of Christ to those whose lives were crushed in a world of sorrow and sin. The reign of Queen Victoria was to see the rise of countless Societies with benevolent and charitable objects. This in itself was a phenomenon which owed far more to the inspiration of his life and work than can be measured. He was himself President or Vice-President or Chairman of a host of Societies, and in constant demand as chairman or speaker at their great May meetings. When he took his seat in the House of Lords, he had described himself as 'an Evangelical of the Evangelicals'; twenty five years in the House of Commons had established his position as their leading spokesman. When he died in 1885, he had been for fifty years since the death of Charles Simeon their undisputed leader in all that was best in their cause in Church and State. The streets of London were filled with mourners as his funeral procession passed by; nothing like it had been seen since that of the Duke of Wellington.

Shaftesbury's death marked the end of an era in the evolution of the Evangelical movement. It could hardly be denied that Evangelical Churchmen had come to hold a unique place in the life of Victorian England. Their real strength lay in their unreserved commitment to the Lordship of Christ as the only Saviour. They were a home loving, Bible reading, Church going, Sunday keeping people, and the seriousness which was the great hall-mark of that generation was the product of their discipline in life and their diligence at work. Their great primary emphasis was on the need for personal conversion and practical holiness; the main focus of their ministry was their sense of vocation as preachers and pastors; their most creative enterprise was their missionary work for the spread of the gospel throughout the world. But Wilberforce and Shaftesbury had taught them as well to combine with their gospel proclamation and their missionary concern what the Hammonds called 'a wide range of social pity';[81] pity which sprang from the compelling power of compassion and the urgent need for remedial action on behalf of others. The great driving motive in all their work was a profound sense of Christian compassion; what they had done for the least of the black slaves in the West Indies or the white slaves in the mills and mines of northern England, they had done for Him. That is why they had won recognition and held the trust of their fellow Churchmen in all the great issues that rose to the surface in their generation. Much land remained to be possessed; others would learn to share in the task of charitable work and missionary endeavour. But there can be no doubt that their labours had made England a cleaner and sweeter and more wholesome country than it had been at the turn of the century. Nor was that all. They were reaching out to touch the ends of the earth for Christ, and their strength had not yet been spent.

But the years that followed Shaftesbury's death were to see a sad diminution in their overall effective influence. This stemmed from the subtle process of change both in the world and in the church at large. The problems with which old-fashioned Evangelicals had to contend had changed in a bewildering manner. The shallow Deism and moral laxity of the Age of Reason had gone; the slave trade had been done away and slaves were free; the merciless exploitation of women and children had been exposed and brought under a measure of control; the lot of the poor and down-trodden had been to some extent ameliorated. But Evangelical Churchmen were viewed with dislike or disgust in many quarters. Edward White Benson, whose father had been a strong Evangelical and who was soon to become Archbishop of Canterbury, wrote off contemporary Evangelicals in a patronizing way in 1883. 'They are all right,' he said; 'they hold nothing but the truth, and they hold it strongly, consistently, sweetly, but with just a little tinge of Torquemada…They are happy in the Court of Israel and of the Women. They have never seen the Court of the Priests'[82] A major challenge had been thrown up by the upsurge of Ritualism and Liberalism in the sixties. Ritualism was the outgrowth of the Tractarian Movement; it proved to be the most discordant and most disruptive force at work in the Church during those years. The English Church Union (1859) on the one hand and the Church Association (1865) on the other hand were to polarize Anglo-Catholics and Evangelicals in controversy and litigation; it was bitter, painful and inconclusive in results. Liberalism had burst on the scene with Darwin's Origin of Species in 1859, with Essays and Reviews in 1860, and with Colenso's book on the Pentateuch in 1862. All this led to acute concern because of its threat to conservative understanding of the inspiration and integrity of Holy Scripture. How was Evangelical continuity to be maintained?

There was no truly national figure to take up the mantle of leadership when Shaftesbury died, but the man who came to the fore in the closing years of the century was John Charles Ryle, 1816–1900. He spent thirty six years as a country vicar in two Suffolk livings and dedicated his leisure to reading and writing. He made himself at home in the theology of Reformers and Puritans, and took special delight in the Fathers of the Evangelical Movement. He soon found a wider outlet for his spiritual concern through his penny tracts whose circulation was counted in millions, and his books which dealt with all the great issues under debate in the sixties and seventies. He was outspoken in his rejection of doctrine and practice which he believed to be inconsistent with or inimical to the Reformation. He was just as quick to perceive that Evangelical clergy were inclined to withdraw from the mainstream of church affairs; they were content to exercise their ministry in backwaters where they hoped to avoid the ebb and flow of conflict and debate. He was determined to make their voice heard in the pulpit, on the platform, through the church press, and to rally their strength in the face of hostile criticism. His appointment in 1880 as the first Bishop of Liverpool was welcomed by Evangelicals everywhere, but was bitterly assailed in the Church Times and by men like Lord Halifax. 'I come among you a Protestant and an Evangelical', Ryle told The Bishopric Committee; 'but…I come with a desire to hold out the right hand to all loyal Churchmen.'[83] In this spirit, he took up his work, and for twenty years strove through good report and ill report to be the just and patient friend of clergy and laymen alike. His great concern was to provide for more living agents, parish churches, and mission halls so that the gospel might be made known among those who had been entirely neglected. And beyond Liverpool, he was known as an 'old soldier' whose courage was equal to the day of battle; a born leader whose virile faith and steadfast purpose brought new hope to younger comrades until his voice was stilled in death in June 1900.

Hardly more than six months later, the old Queen's life moved to a close: it was January 1901, and it was the passing of an epoch. She had never had any great liking for Evangelicals or Anglo-Catholics; her own favourites were all middle-of-the-road ecclesiastics, ranging from Samuel Wilberforce to Randall Davidson. Her long reign had seen a vast change in the moral and spiritual tone of England, although this had faltered in her last years. Its values had become much more shallow and its way of life more worldly. Edward VII was to personify the more vulgar spirit of pleasure seeking and money making in the new century. Evangelicals were to find that more than ever they would have their backs to the wall in the struggle with Ritualism and Liberalism. When the Royal Commission on Ecclesiastical Discipline brought down its report in 1906, the train was laid for the preparation of a Revised Prayer Book. It soon became clear that the crux would lie in the use of vestments and the practice of some form of Reservation. Controversy was to gather ever increasing momentum until Europe went up in flames and four years of war put their brake on the wheels of debate. Nor was that all. Evangelicals had found it hard enough to come to terms with the incipient Liberalism of Essays and Reviews in 1860 and Lux Mundi in 1889; they were even more confused or dismayed when the liberalism of the Victorian era blossomed into the Modernism of the twentieth century. There had been one great lack in their earlier history; they had failed to promote serious scholarship at the highest level. It was left for middle Churchmen like J.B. Lightfoot and B.F. Westcott to explore the validity of historical and textual criticism. Evangelicals were to find themselves at a grave disadvantage when in due course they were called to reckon with the so-called assured results of a highly technical form of scholarship. There were many hidden pitfalls and many spiritual uncertainties in the path of the Evangelical as he stood on the threshold of a new century.

Who would stand out as the leading contemporary Evangelical in the early decades of that darkening century? There were many clergy who sought to walk in the old paths, but their voice was not heard beyond their own parish borders. There were some in places of influence and leadership who were known and loved as men of saintly life and purpose: such men as F.J. Chavasse of Liverpool and H.C.G. Moule of Durham. But the special role that Ryle had filled as guardian and advocate of the doctrines of the Reformation was to fall to Edmund Arbuthnott Knox. Oxford had been his home until 1884 and his experience as a College Fellow, Tutor, and Dean was to prove an invaluable training ground for his future. The whole spiritual climate had changed since the first phase of the Oxford Movement and he could not remain indifferent to the rapid growth of Ritualism. He had also felt the chill wind of the Liberalism in an Oxford which was increasingly susceptible to the theology of Strauss and Baur. But he had left Oxford late in 1884 and had spent ten years in parish work. This was followed by his Consecration in 1894 as Bishop Suffragan of Coventry in the still undivided Diocese of Worcester, and then by his appointment in 1903 as Bishop of Manchester. His great ability in organization and administration soon proved itself in the ordeal of sheer hard work. He strove to unite his clergy on the basis of loyal conformity to the *Book of Common Prayer* and this constrained him at length to announce that he would not license any curate to a parish in which vestments remained in use. He led the opposition in the Upper House of Convocation at York to the compromise suggestion that a white chasuble might be worn by the chief minister at the Holy Communion, and the swelling debate on the practice of Reservation led him to publish his book on Sacrifice or Sacrament. He retired from Manchester in 1920, but remained in the forefront of Evangelical circles until his death in 1937. That was the passing of their most influential leader for a generation after the death of Ryle.

Nonetheless apart from Knox, Moule, Chavasse, and a few others, where were the Evangelicals in the first quarter of the twentieth century? There was no one who had the same outstanding flair for leadership or the same commanding influence as Ryle; no one who had the same disciplined strength of intellect or the same inborn authority as Knox. Even the General Secretary of the Church Missionary Society lamented to Archbishop Davidson as early as in 1911 that 'there are so few leaders in what are known as the Evangelical ranks.'[84] Pietism was the haven into which many had begun to retreat, a haven whose centre was the annual Convention for the deepening of spiritual life held each year at Keswick. But the Evangelical cause at grass roots level was in better shape than was commonly recognized. The May meetings of the Societies were the rallying-point which drew Evangelicals together in their common concern for the furtherance of the gospel. The Church Pastoral Aid

Society was as vigorous and progressive as ever. Trusts like Simeon's Foundation still controlled the appointment and secured the succession to many livings. And their real strength was still to be seen in the life and work of the parish clergy. This was the sphere in which their grand purpose to win souls for God had to be fulfilled. They may have had a hard row to plow in an age when Edwardian secularism was suddenly overshadowed by the appalling destruction of the Great War. But they stuck to their task; they tilled the ground; they sowed the seed. This was seen in their Scriptural discipline, their personal godliness, their pastoral devotion; it was seen in their reverent submission to truth, their intimate fellowship with God, their diligent compassion for men. Their great legacy to the post-war generation was to teach men to bow low in continual obedience before the Word of God and the Lordship of Christ, that so doing, they might learn which are the old paths they must not forsake and which are the new they must explore.

6

Bishop Lightfoot
and
New Testament Scholarship

Material for a life of Bishop Lightfoot is slender and scattered. There was no two-volume biography as in the case of his friends, Westcott, Benson and Hort, perhaps because he had never married and had neither son nor daughter to take up such a task. Bishop Eden noted that there was no biography at Lightfoot's 'own earnest desire'.[85] But F.J.A. Hort wrote an article for the *Dictionary of National Biography* which was published shortly before Hort's death in 1892. Then an anonymous article, generally ascribed to H.W. Watkins, appeared in the *Quarterly Review* in January 1893 and was reprinted in book form with a Preface by Westcott in 1894.[86] H.C.G. Moule paid a moving tribute in his sermon on 'Wise Men and Scribes' in 1907, and again in his lecture on 'My Cambridge Classical Teachers' in

1913. Forty-three years after Lightfoot's death, G.E. Eden and F.C. Macdonald in 1932 edited a small book with the title *Lightfoot of Durham*. This was a labour of love at the hands of those who had been Sons of the House, drawing from their private stores of memory and affection to furnish us with what J.A.T. Robinson called 'irreplaceable material'.[87] The years passed by until 1964 when Stephen Neill's *Interpretation of the New Testament, 1861-1961*, gave a striking account of the value of Lightfoot's work on *The Apostolic Fathers*. This was followed in 1971 by C.K. Barrett's paper on Joseph Barber Lightfoot read to the Durham University Lightfoot Society, with a critical assessment of Lightfoot's exegesis of the Pauline Letters. Then in 1981, John A.T. Robinson delivered a Durham Cathedral Lecture on Joseph Barber Lightfoot, with a delightful mixture of light-hearted anecdote and serious discussion.

There are also many references to Lightfoot scattered through other biographies, of which none is of more value than the *Life of Edward White Benson*, which was published in 1899. There is nothing original in the pages that now follow; they draw freely on the sources available to me in order to provide an orderly chronological narrative.

Joseph Barber Lightfoot was 'a child of the north',[88] born on April 13th 1828 in his father's home at 84 Duke Street, Liverpool. The slave-trade in the eighteenth century had seen Liverpool grow from a small seaside village to a large and thriving seaport; it was surpassed only by London and Bristol. Abolition of the slave-trade in 1807 had hardly affected Liverpool's continued importance as the main point of entry for the cotton imports for the mills in northern England. There was a strong Protestant element in the population that lined the banks of the

Mersey, though migrant workers from Ireland were to bring in as well a strong Roman Catholic leavening. Lightfoot was one of four children: he had two sisters, and an older brother who was in due course to be ordained. But he was a delicate child and was taught at home by private tutors until he was twelve years old. Then he spent two years at the Liverpool Royal Institution; but no details are now available. A school friend was to write in the *Cambridge Review* on January 23rd 1890: 'His life from childhood seems to have been strictly of one piece, pervaded by one continuous thread of earnest duty, plain uprightness, and scrupulous fidelity. The very idea that Lightfoot in any circumstance at school or college could have been untrue to his own high standard of resolve and aim is to me inconceivable.'[89] Lightfoot's father died in 1843, but no record survives to tell how this bereavement affected the fifteen-year-old boy. All that is known is that in January 1844 his mother moved with her family from their home at Tranmere to a new home 'a little way out of Birmingham'.[90] Did he miss Liverpool? A year or two later, on holiday in Liverpool, there was perhaps a touch of whimsical nostalgia in writing to Benson: 'Liverpool is really a lovely place and only lacks your angelic self to make it a complete Paradise.'[91]

Lightfoot was sent to King Edward VI's School in Birmingham and at once came under James Prince Lee, who was to have a decisive influence upon his life. James Prince Lee had been the second of Thomas Arnold's appointments to the staff at Rugby and was the first of Arnold's men to leave Rugby for a headmastership. He was one of Arnold's idealists who strove to make godliness and good learning the guiding principles of their teaching.

James Prince Lee was born in 1804, went up to Trinity College Cambridge in 1824, and joined Arnold's staff in 1830. He was a greater classical scholar than Arnold, but he admired Arnold enormously and followed his example in using the Classics to stimulate wider reading. He came to King Edward's School in 1838, and had astonishing success in the not quite ten years during which he remained. Thirteen of his pupils were to obtain first class honours in the Classical Tripos at Cambridge; five were Senior Classics; eight were College Fellows; twelve took Holy Orders. What Hort described as his 'many-sided intellect and religious fervour' had a profound effect on the boys whom he taught.[92] Benson told his son that 'Lee was the greatest man I have ever come within the influence of—the greatest and the best.'[93] After Lee's death in 1869, Benson wrote to Lightfoot: 'When we think of the rapt way in which we used to stand listening to his Georgics and his Thucydides, and the spin with which he sent us home day by day at 14 years old!!'[94] This was the man under whom Lightfoot was to complete his schooldays. 'I have sometimes thought', so he wrote after Lee's death, 'that if I were allowed to have one hour only of my past life over again, I would choose a Butler lesson under Lee.'[95] But the consummation of Lee's teaching came in sessions on the Greek New Testament, to which Lightfoot subsequently traced 'his enthusiasm for those studies in which he became pre-eminent.'[96]

If the inspiration of James Prince Lee as a superb Classics master was the first great force in Lightfoot's school life, barely second was the lifelong friendship which he formed with Edward White Benson as a fellow schoolboy. In 1882 Lightfoot was in the Chair at a dinner held in Benson's honour on his appointment to Canterbury. He was overcome with a surge of emotion as he proposed Benson's health. 'Trembling all over and with tears streaming down his face, Lightfoot told us how on the very first day of his entering King Edward's School, Benson...showed him much kindness and walked home with him.'[97] Benson had been at King Edward's School since 1840, but was a year younger than his new friend. He soon came to know and admire Lightfoot's immense capacity for work, as well as the brilliance with which it was performed. Lightfoot took little part in games, perhaps because of his health; as a result he read far more widely than was required, and his knowledge used to reveal itself in the class room through his incidental comments. 'We hear of the boys' astonishment and their master's delight at indications of his private reading.'[98] Hort said that he had a cheerful temper, much dry humour, and a certain quaintness of manner.[99] He and Benson were inseparable; all their leisure was spent in one another's company. Strange as it sounds today, they went walking on half-holidays and read Greek plays together. Lightfoot went up to Cambridge in October 1847, leaving Benson to complete one more year at school. It was during that year, in January 1848, that to Benson's sorrow Lee left King Edward's School to become Bishop of Manchester. Meanwhile the two friends had embarked on a voluminous correspondence; their letters were remarkable for their freshness and their playful banter, as well as the high tone of their serious discussion as they shared their intellectual discoveries and their spiritual enthusiasms.

Lightfoot went up to Trinity College Cambridge as a pensioner in October 1847. There he soon came to know

Brooke Foss Westcott (1825-1901), who had been at King Edward's School from 1837 to 1844. Lightfoot wrote of him to Benson in March 1848 with unbounded enthusiasm: 'The object of my greatest admiration is Westcott. I shall not attempt to tell you all his good qualities, for that would not be very possible, but imagine to yourself one of the most gentlemanly, quietest, humblest, and most conscientious of mankind! (to say nothing of cleverness), and you have my opinion of him.'[100] Westcott graduated in 1848 as twenty-fourth Wrangler and topped the list in the first class of the Classical Tripos. He became a Fellow of Trinity in 1849 and began to take private pupils. Among them were Lightfoot, Hort and Benson. Fenton John Anthony Hort (1828-1892) had been at Rugby under Arnold and Tait from 1841 to 1846, and then went up to Trinity College as a pensioner a year ahead of Lightfoot. Edward White Benson (1829-1896) followed Lightfoot to Trinity as a sub-sizar in October 1848. Lightfoot and Benson soon began to breakfast with each other on Sunday mornings; they had a veal-and-ham pie, and then settled down to read from the Fathers. 'This', wrote Arthur Benson, 'was my father's first introduction to Cyprian whose *De Unitate* they read and discussed.'[101] Lightfoot, Hort and Benson all read Classics under Westcott during those years, and the intimacy thus formed was to bind them into lifelong friendship. Lightfoot became a Scholar of Trinity in 1849, graduated in 1851 as thirtieth Wrangler and Senior Classic, and was the first of the two Chancellor's Medallists. 'It soon became part of the legend that...he had written all his Tripos papers without a single error.'[102] Hort was third in the first class of the Classical Tripos in 1850, and Benson eighth in 1852. The presence and friendship of these four men at the same time and in the same College was in itself remarkable; they were to serve the Church with the highest distinction until the end of the century.

Lightfoot and Hort were both elected as Fellows of Trinity in 1852, but the quartet gradually broke up. Westcott became a Master at Harrow in 1852 and Benson at Rugby in 1853, while Hort became vicar of a little parish near Hitchin in 1857. Lightfoot spent the fifties in the customary routine for a College Fellow. He pursued his private reading; he took special pupils; he gave College lectures. In 1853 he won the Norrisian Prize; in 1854 he was made a Deacon by James Prince Lee on his title as a Fellow; in 1857 he was appointed as one of the three College Tutors; and in 1858 he was ordained by James Prince Lee to the Priesthood. His College lectures were chiefly on the works of Herodotus, Euripides and Aeschylus, but also on the Greek text of the New Testament. He was too shy to initiate conversation, but was always eager to respond when others made the advance. Sometimes he took a few pupils with him for a reading party in the long vacation, and gave them all the help he could in their field of work. It is said that he would relax by running with the boats on the river: 'You can get a good run there', so he claimed, 'without being thought a perfect lunatic.'[103] It was probably during these years that he spent a holiday in Switzerland: he made his way to the top of the Jungfrau and back in a single walk from the Rhone valley, accompanied only by a shoemaker from the village of Fiesch.[104] And in 1854 he and Benson made a visit to Rome, where they were received by the Pope.[105] But he was much less drawn to ornate ritual of any kind than Benson and was much more moderate in his churchmanship. Even as early as in March 1848 he had written: 'I am not at all settled in my Church views, that is in matters of the so-called high and low Church parties; the more I read on the subject, the less fixed I become; and I should be heartily thankful if I saw any prospect of coming to a decided conclusion on such points...One thing I am at present certain of, that I could not entertain such uncharitable views as those held by the extreme (so-called) high Church party.'[106]

It must have been during these years that he became engrossed in the Apostolic Fathers. This is clear from what he wrote in 1885 in his Preface to his work on St. Ignatius: 'The subject has been before me for nearly thirty years.' He had begun to acquire a unique reputation for his lectures on the Pauline Epistles; this was enhanced by his articles and reviews in the *Journal of Classical and Sacred Philology*. Perhaps his most significant contribution was a review of Benjamin Jowett's commentary on Romans, Galatians and Thessalonians, and A. P. Stanley's commentary on Corinthians. Lightfoot drew attention to the importance of these works as the first serious attempt to apply German methods of textual criticism in English commentaries. Stanley referred to this review in a letter which he wrote to Bishop Tait of London on October 12th 1856 concerning Tait's choice of an Examining Chaplain. 'One other Cambridge name occurs to me—Lightfoot, Fellow and, I think, Tutor of Trinity of the same stamp as Westcott and Benson, but with the advantage of having a more independent position. All I know of him is an article in the *Cambridge Philological Review*, which contained an attack on the scholarship and accents of my book on the Corinthians, but was written with great candour and kindness, as was also a correspondence consequent thereon.'[107] Tait did not appoint Lightfoot at the time; but he did not forget. Lightfoot became one of his Examining Chaplains in 1862 and, on Tait's appointment to Canterbury in 1869, Lightfoot wrote to him in memorable terms. 'Looking to the future of the English Church at a great crisis in her history, I can not but feel most deeply thankful for the appointment...Alas! there is one sad thought connected with an event which otherwise would have given unmingled joy: the pleasant associations connected with Fulham must now become memories.'[108] But the work at Fulham was renewed at Lambeth; Lightfoot served Tait as an Examining Chaplain until his own appointment to Durham in 1879.

Lightfoot's College rooms were Isaac Newton's old set, E4, in the Great Court. H.C.G. Moule called on him there, in June 1860, and asked to be entered on his list of freshmen in the coming October. 'Desperately shy was I', Moule recalled more than fifty years later. 'And he, if I do not mistake, felt a little shy too, for it was his nature so to be.'[109] Moule's first year as an undergraduate was Lightfoot's last year as a College Tutor; but that short year made an impression and left an influence upon his mind and heart that was to last for life. Moule never forgot Lightfoot's readings in Aeschylus or the strength and freshness of his Chapel sermons. But the influence which he exercised did not reside chiefly in his superb skill in the Greek text of Aeschylus or the Pauline letters; it sprang from the magnetism of what he was, and the 'kindness which looked always through his reserve'[110]. In a Commemoration Sermon in the Chapel of Trinity College on December 10th 1907, Moule's words glowed with the warmth of remembered thankfulness as he spoke of Lightfoot: 'To watch his simple but profound devotion day by day in this Chapel, to see a little of his splendid diligence in toil and duty,…to know by a sure instinct, as we talked about him or heard rumours of him, that he was always and everywhere the same,…all this meant for us a perpetual moral impression of the sort to tell, just at our time of life, for the purest and most lasting good.'[111] Both in this sermon and in an address at Newcastle-upon-Tyne on February 22nd 1913, Moule drew Lightfoot's picture as his Tutor in unforgettable terms: 'No man ever loitered so late in the Great Court that he did not see Lightfoot's lamp burning in his study window; though no man either was so regularly present in morning Chapel at seven o'clock that he did not find Lightfoot always there with him.'[112]

In 1861, Lightfoot succeeded C.J. Ellicott as Hulsean Professor of Divinity and began his great series of New Testament lectures, concentrating on the Pauline Letters. Cambridge had known nothing like them for their power of original thought and pellucid expression. Men were so eager to hear him that the largest lecture room soon proved inadequate and the lectures were then transferred to the Great Hall of Trinity College. The Master of Trinity was to describe the passage between the Senate House and Caius College as 'black with the fluttering gowns of students' as they hurried 'to imbibe…a knowledge of the New Testament such as was not open to their less happy predecessors.'[113] Recognition of his gifted contribution to the life of Cambridge quickly escalated. In 1860 he had been elected for a four-year term as a member of the new 'Council of the Senate'; three times he was to be re-elected, so that with only one two-year interval, he served from

1860 to 1878. In 1861 he was chosen as a Chaplain for the Prince Consort as Chancellor of the University, and then as a Tutor for the Prince of Wales during his brief residence in Trinity. In 1862 he became a Chaplain for Queen Victoria, and in due course this led to his appointment as Deputy Clerk of the Closet. He had taken his Master's degree in 1854, knowing that twelve years were meant to elapse before he could proceed to a Doctorate; but by a special Grace of the Senate in 1864, he was made a Doctor of Divinity two years ahead of time. His love for Cambridge was seen in 1870 when he transferred to the University a sum of £4,500 for the foundation of three scholarships to encourage the study of ecclesiastical history. Meanwhile his habits of study remained just as Moule had seen in 1860. 'About six o'clock', so Bishop Eden recalled in 1929, 'his door was shut for study that went on often into the early morning hours.'[114]

Lightfoot's New Testament lectures were to issue in three magnificent commentaries: Galatians in 1865; Philippians in 1868; Colossians and Philemon in 1875. 'His independence of predecessors was startling', Armitage Robinson declared. 'Wordsworth we knew; Alford we knew; Ellicott we knew; but nothing like this had appeared.'[115] One great innovation was his diligent recension of the Greek text. 'I was encouraged', so he wrote in the Preface to Galatians, 'by the promise of assistance from my friends the Rev. B.F. Westcott and the Rev. F.J.A. Hort, who are engaged in a joint recension of the Greek Testament and have revised the text of this Epistle for my use. Though I have ventured to differ from them in some passages and hold myself finally responsible in all, I am greatly indebted to them.'[116] The other great innovation was to insist on the historical context of the original Letters. It was his great desire to see the man who wrote these Letters and to know their background. He introduced each paragraph with a brief but vigorous summary and then furnished notes on each verse; the notes were marked by his terse and sturdy common sense as well as by his solid learning. This set his work apart from that of all others, even that of his friend Westcott. William Sanday said that neither Oxford nor Germany could show anything to match Lightfoot for 'exactness of scholarship, width of erudition, scientific method, sobriety of judgment and lucidity of style.'[117] All three commentaries were accompanied by lengthy dissertations: two in the case of Philippians, but three each in Galatians and Colossians. The most famous were the dissertations on 'St Paul and The Three' in Galatians and on 'The Christian Ministry' in Philippians. Lightfoot argued that the only correct way in which to treat these matters was to examine their history. He approached the problems of theology on historical lines and resolved them on historical grounds; and he was a pioneer in this kind of scientific historical research into the New Testament origins of the Christian ministry.

Lightfoot's Preface to the first edition of Galatians began with the statement: 'The present work is intended to form part of a complete edition of St Paul's Epistles.'[118] But that plan was never fulfilled. The series was interrupted after 1868; seven years elapsed before Colossians appeared; then the series came to an end. 'A few fragments...gathered from lecture notes' were published by the Lightfoot Trustees in 1895 as 'Notes on Epistles of St Paul from Unpublished Commentaries'. There was only enough to deepen regret that his pen had been for ever laid aside.[119]

But the three great commentaries which were finished had forged a new standard for all future commentaries. Their impact was immediate and enormous. Galatians reached its tenth edition in 1890; Philippians in 1890; and Colossians in 1882. More than any other, more than Westcott and more than Hort, Lightfoot was the founder of that school of scientific exegesis for which Cambridge was to become famous. If more recent commentaries do not refer back to Lightfoot as much as was the case at least until 1950, it is largely because his work has been absorbed to an extent which makes recent writers the less aware of their indebtedness to him. It is true that his views on some matters have now lost ground in the light of later research. Thus he argued strongly for the North Galatian theory before Sir William Ramsay's labours in Asia Minor did so much to strengthen the South Galatian theory. His view of the time and the place and the order of the Prison Letters has also been challenged. But the main fact remains; his work has stood the test of time; he was an exegete par excellence. It was through the genius of his scholarship that the Cambridge school of New Testament studies won an unrivalled eminence before the close of the Victorian era.

Meanwhile the most serious attack on the integrity of the New Testament was to develop in the sixties as a result of the work of Ferdinand Christian Baur and his colleagues in the Tübingen school in Germany. Baur had set out to rewrite the whole story of the early church on the strength of his hypothesis that the two great apostles, Peter and Paul, were at fatal loggerheads. This led him to argue that the New Testament was no more than a brilliant attempt to conceal their fundamental opposition. Lightfoot had been aware of the dangerous influence of these German scholars since the fifties, and had become convinced that such historical problems could only be resolved by a severe study of New Testament texts in relation to 'the whole corpus of Christian literature in the first two centuries.'[120] This led him to suspend his series of commentaries after 1868 in order to embark on a critical edition of *The Apostolic Fathers*. Thus in July 1869 he brought out his great work *S. Clement of Rome: The Two Epistles to the Corinthians*. He had begun with Clement because his Letters were the earliest extant writings outside the New Testament, and he edited them with the same diligent attention to textual criticism, the same careful exegesis, and the same kind of introduction as in his commentaries.[121] But in 1869 there was only one imperfect manuscript of the two Epistles; this was in the Codex Alexandrinus at the British Museum. The situation was radically altered some years later with the discovery of the missing sections of both Letters. Metropolitan Byrennios published the complete text from a manuscript at Constantinople in 1875, and the Cambridge University Library purchased a manuscript of the Syriac New Testament including 1 and 2 Clement in 1876. Lightfoot at once began to prepare a second volume which came out in 1877 as a supplement to his earlier edition. He had almost completed a full-scale revision of both volumes before he died in 1889. It was published with a Preface by Westcott in 1890 as the first two volumes of his monumental *Apostolic Fathers*.

Lightfoot's friendship with Benson had continued unabated throughout the sixties although their life and work lay in different directions. Benson remained on the staff at Rugby until 1859; then he became the foundation headmaster of Wellington. His correspondence with Lightfoot was as fresh and lively as ever. 'I do not believe', Lightfoot was later to say, 'there has been a thought or wish in the mind or heart of either which he has not shared with the other.'[122] Benson asked Lightfoot and Temple to be the Godparents for his first-born, Martin White Benson, in 1857.[123] He told Westcott on October 28th 1864 of a curious encounter with Lightfoot at Winchester.

> It was most amusing to see him rush headlong into the Cloisters at Winchester one day soon after we parted from you. My wife and I were sitting there at the time, not having the least idea of his propinquity, nor he of ours. The vain attempts he made to see through his eye-glass until within about a yard of us, and his difficulty in believing his eyes when he did see, rendered him funny.[124]

An even more interesting sidelight on Lightfoot's character occurs in Arthur Benson's account of a holiday excursion in 1866. 'Westcott and Lightfoot joined in a summer expedition with ourselves at Llanfairfachan. As we drove the last stage of our journey in a coach, Lightfoot was engrossed in a novel of Jane Austen's, laughing as he read, with the rich chuckle that was so characteristic of him, and refusing to look at any of the surrounding scenery.'[125] Two years later the same party took two adjacent houses in Langland Bay near Swansea.[126] And on January 4th 1870, Benson, Lightfoot and Westcott 'walked over Derwentwater on the ice to near the Islands, then turned across and went up Catbells in the snow—a most glorious walk—a fine stormy sky with still golden lights catching the hills.'[127]

Lightfoot had remained at Cambridge when first Westcott and then Hort went elsewhere as each in turn had been married. But in 1870 Lightfoot stood aside when the Regius Professorship fell vacant, in order to make room for Westcott and so bring him back to Cambridge. Then in 1872 Hort was able to return to Cambridge as a Fellow of Emmanuel with a lectureship in theology. In 1875 Lightfoot became Lady Margaret Professor of Divinity, and in 1878 Hort was elected as Hulsean Professor in succession to J. J. S. Perowne. So throughout the seventies the three friends worked side by side to foster a school of New Testament scholarship which has had no equal. All three had been Fellows of Trinity; they were all steeped in the Greek and Latin Classics; and for one year, 1878–9, they held all three Chairs of Divinity. After Westcott's return, he and Lightfoot used to meet for 'the 4:30 dinner in Hall, which almost alone they somewhat anti-socially kept up so that Lightfoot could' then retire and 'work through the night'.[128] Moule has left one delightful anecdote, drawn from his time as Dean of Trinity between 1873 and 1877. 'One remembrance I cherish', so he wrote, 'is of a day…when I was Dean and…had to take the Chair. On one side of me sat Westcott, and Lightfoot on the other, and a most characteristic talk they had about Skénos (Tabernacle) in 2 Cor. 5:1.'[129] In 1872 Lightfoot and Westcott signed an elaborate statement to urge disuse of the damnatory clauses in the Athanasian Creed.[130] In 1877 Lightfoot was nominated by the Universities of Oxford and Cambridge as one of the seven Commissioners to revise the University's Statutes for Cambridge. He was also largely instrumental in introducing the Theological Tripos at Cambridge and in establishing a University College in Liverpool. The hard grind of nightly study never narrowed the breadth of his concern for the welfare both of the Church and of Cambridge.

Lightfoot was one of the first to vindicate the character of New Testament Greek as the lingua franca of the Graeco-Roman world of that age. He had maintained ever since March 1856 in his Review of Recent Editions of St Paul's Epistles that the late Greek in which the New Testament was written was as precise as the classical Attic; there is nothing that could imply that St Paul had an imperfect knowledge of the language or was deficient in the skill with which he used it. He was more than pleased when his friends Westcott and Hort embarked on a scheme to produce a critical edition of the Greek text, and their work was to form the basic text for his three great commentaries. But it was to be of cardinal importance for another undertaking. The Convocation of Canterbury in 1870 set in motion a plan for the revision of the Authorised Version of the Bible, and the three friends, Lightfoot, Westcott and Hort, were all original members of the New Testament Company of Revisers. Shortly before their work began, Lightfoot read a paper on the subject to a clerical society; this was later published with the title *On a Fresh Revision of the English New Testament*. The Company of Revisers began their work in June 1870; their work went on until November 1880. 'As a rule, a session of four days (was) held every month, with the exception of August and September' throughout the whole ten years; that is, forty days each year, year in and year out, from which Lightfoot was seldom absent.[131] Hort, who must have known the facts, said that the general character of the revision was in no small measure determined at the very first session by Lightfoot's argument against acquiescence in the use of an unrevised edition of the Greek text. Westcott and Hort devoted every available moment to their critical edition of the Greek text, and their work kept pace with that of the new English translation. Their edition of the Greek New Testament appeared at length on May 12th 1881 and the Revised Version of the English New Testament on May 17th.

A still wider call on Lightfoot's time and strength was to coincide with the seventies; for in 1871 he became a Canon of St Paul's Cathedral. This led to a very close association with two men of exceptional ability: R.W. Church, who was the Dean, and H.P. Liddon, who was one of the best known preachers of the day. Church and Liddon were both Tractarians in training and outlook, but they came to value Lightfoot's role on the Chapter and in the pulpit in the highest degree. As for Lightfoot, he threw himself with his accustomed energy into all the demands of his office, and it was to call forth all his gifts as a preacher. Tait said that in the past Lightfoot had been 'rather heavy', but that at St Paul's he proved an 'extraordinarily eloquent preacher'.[132] Canon Scott Holland spoke of 'his glowing ardour of speech'; it sprang from his inmost being.[133] 'Before long', Hort wrote, 'large congregations filled the Cathedral when it was his turn to occupy the pulpit.'[134] But his appeal as a preacher was not to make itself felt to the utmost advantage until the time came when he had to address his ordinands in Durham. It was then said that his perfect simplicity opened the door for a new and telling style of preaching: 'deep truths...alive with meaning because they were the manifest transcript of his own experience'.[135] He did not often speak of his own experience, but at times his voice would falter and tears rolled down his cheeks. This may still be perceived in a moving address which he delivered as the first of a series at Cuddesdon, with the overtones of a personal apologia: 'You will possibly say, What does he himself that speaks these things to us? Alas, I am ashamed to tell you. All I dare say is this. I think I see the beauty of holiness, and am enamoured of it, though I attain it not, and howsoever little I attain, would rather live and die in the pursuit of it than in the pursuit…of all the advantages that this world affords.'[136]

During these years Lightfoot was drawn into public controversy on a matter which was directly connected with the radical rewriting of early Christian history by the Tübingen school in Germany. A book appeared in 1874 under the veil of anonymity with the title *Supernatural Religion*. It set out to argue in view of Baur's reconstruction of early Christian history that 'the Gospels are so far removed in point of time from the events they purport to record that they are in fact historically worthless.'[137] This book had a great vogue when it first found a place in the market. It was rumoured that the author was the learned Bishop J.C. Thirlwall; it was in fact written by a minor figure whose name was J.C. Cassels. That was bad enough, but not enough to have provoked Lightfoot if it had not also impugned Westcott's integrity as a scholar. Cassels had accused Westcott of deliberate mistranslation of a passage in Irenaeus in order to support his conservative view of the New Testament. Lightfoot was so incensed at this attack that he went through the book 'with the same blue pencil he had used on undergraduate attempts at Greek and Latin unseens'.[138] He wrote a series of nine articles for the Contemporary Review between December 1874 and May 1877; they were subsequently republished in May 1889 as Essays on a Work Entitled Supernatural Religion. As a result, Cassels' book was so discredited that it could no longer command a sale. Lightfoot had no difficulty in its refutation; but he did more. His Essays 'survey the second century evidence for the origin and circulation of the gospels, and do a good deal to establish the trustworthiness of…Ignatius, Polycarp and Irenaeus… It contains the essence of the argument more formidably expressed in the three-volume edition of Ignatius and Polycarp.'[139] Stephen Neill said that it was 'the best controversial writing in English since Bentley wrote on the Letters of Phalaris' in 1699.[140]

In 1867 Lightfoot had declined the offer of the See of Lichfield; then in January 1879 he received an invitation to accept the See of Durham. He went through deep waters before he could ground his reply on terra firma. Dean Church said that no one could take his place were he to leave Cambridge; but what ought he to do? 'I do not know how he will decide; tomorrow I suppose he will settle. He is still perplexed. But if he goes to Durham, Bishop Butler will have a successor worthy of him in the combination of innocence, simplicity, and pure nobleness of thought and purpose with intellectual forces which make his fellows wonder and admire.'[141] At last there came what Lightfoot was to describe as 'that long wakeful night when the decision was finally made'.[142] In the morning, on January 27th, he wrote to Westcott: 'At length I have sent my answer 'Yes'. It seemed to me that to resist any longer would be Theomachein (to fight against God). My consolation and my hope for the future is that it has cost me the greatest moral effort, the greatest venture of faith which I ever made.'[143] Archbishop Tait recorded in his Diary: 'Lightfoot's appointment to Durham opens a bright prospect; a man of really humble mind, of great learning and perfect scholarship.'[144] His Consecration took place in Westminster Abbey on April 25th; Westcott preached the sermon on Psalm 84:7. The space in the Abbey was too small to admit all those who came. He was enthroned in Durham Cathedral on May 5th when he preached a striking sermon. 'There was a touch of distinction about him which, coupled with the unique tradition of the Northumbrian Church in which he delighted, seemed to give a special significance to the characteristic northern welcome he received.'[145] On All Saints Day, Benson wrote to Westcott and told him of a 'wonderful visit' to Lightfoot and of Lightfoot's 'joyous solemnity' in his great See.[146]

On his arrival in the Diocese, Lightfoot lodged for eight weeks in the Judges' Rooms in Durham Castle before taking up residence at Bishop Auckland. He embarked at once on a strenuous visitation of the Diocese and in the course of time carried out a visit to almost every parish. He laid down the pattern for his Confirmation Services at which he always gave two addresses. In September 1880 he convened a Diocesan Conference of clergy and laity, the first ever held in Durham, and thereafter it met every two years. His Presidential Address set out what was always his goal: 'A Church is something more than an aggregate of distinct parishes or isolated congregations. The idea of a Church involves the conception of a corporate life. A Church is only a Church in so far as it realizes this conception. To extend the sympathies and motives of common membership beyond the limits of the parish to the limits of the Diocese is to make an important stride in the realization of this idea.'[147] This was reinforced in his two Diocesan Charges in 1882 and 1886; but his first care was the division of the Diocese. This had been in view for some years, but it fell to him to see it through. The Diocese of Newcastle came into being in 1882 and on St James' Day he took part in the Consecration of the first Bishop. He had increased the number of Rural Deaneries and adjusted their boundaries in July 1880, and in May 1882 he divided the single Archdeaconry into two. He launched a Church Building Fund in January 1884 and a general Diocesan Fund in 1886. All his episcopal income was spent for the benefit of the Diocese, and he gave unstinted support to the many extra Diocesan bodies such as the Temperance Society and the Seamens Mission. He ordained 323 Deacons and built 45 new churches or mission chapels. He did much to promote the use of lay readers and lay evangelists and he formed an Association of Women for Church Work. 'I have not been, and never intend to be', he said in October 1889, 'the Bishop of a party, but the Bishop of the Diocese.'[48]

The home for the Bishops of Durham was Auckland Castle, and Lightfoot delighted in its historic splendour. But he was a single man: how could he make the best use of his home for the benefit of the Diocese? The solution first took shape in his mind on 'that wakeful night' when his decision was made. He would make it the home for a small group of men from Oxford and Cambridge who would come for a year prior to their Ordination in his Diocese. They would come as more than pupils; he would look upon them as sons. The first two came with him in 1879; but as a rule there were six or seven men in residence. They were seen as sons of the house; they were his guests; there was never any thought of payment. There was a firm daily routine, which began with morning chapel. There were lectures from 9:00 to 11:00 a.m., and private reading from 11:00 to 1:00 p.m. After lunch they were sent out to engage in parish visitation and other parish duties. They shared every meal and every Chapel Service with the Bishop, and he won their hearts in long walks with them in the grounds of Auckland Castle. On Sunday evenings when church services were over, the sons and the local clergy used to gather in relaxed and informal fellowship. Lightfoot's shyness did not detract from his need or capacity for the affection and confidence of those who were with him, and the value for them of such close and continued intercourse was beyond all calculation. They could only speak of him in superlative language and they never liked to miss the annual reunion on St Peter's Day which took place each year after 1883. There were in all eighty-six sons of the house during his episcopate, and he declared that the men whom he had gathered round him were at the very centre of all his plans for the Diocese.[149] And in 1894 Westcott gave it as his considered opinion that Lightfoot's greatest work could be seen in this band of men trained to bear his spirit to another generation.[150]

Lightfoot combined in rare degree both spiritual stature and mental greatness. No one could fill his place in the ranks of New Testament scholarship and men grieved to think that his duties in Durham would mark the end of his literary labours. He said himself that he had not undertaken oversight of a Diocese only to neglect its duties; only time would reveal whether it were still possible to pursue his work as a scholar.[151] His first years at Auckland Castle saw the daily continuance of his Cambridge routine. He rose in the early morning and lit the fire which had been laid for him overnight. Then he settled down to two or three hours of work in his bedroom before breakfast. It was only in his later years when his health had begun to fail that he reluctantly gave up this plan of work. Sometimes he could devote the end of the morning and as a rule most of the evening to his studies. Every August he went away for a well-deserved holiday when the mornings and the evenings were reserved for study. He took books to read or proof-sheets to correct on his journeys by rail and his long drives in the outlying villages in the Diocese. He never employed an amanuensis; he always verified his own references. His massive learning and prodigious memory were the assets in the background of all his work. Westcott was to say that when a subject had been chosen, Lightfoot 'mastered, stored, arranged in his mind all the materials which were available for its complete treatment'; then wrote rapidly and continuously, drawing on his memory for each reference, only verifying them afterwards at the proof stage.[152] Only those who saw his life day by day could fully appreciate the way in which he snatched every available moment in order to complete his work.[153] What it all meant was seen in the *magnum opus* of his life as a scholar and historian: the three volume edition of *S. Ignatius and S. Polycarp in The Apostolic Fathers*.

Lightfoot had long felt that the one valid counter to the Tübingen theory of New Testament history would lie in a rigorous appraisal of sub-apostolic literature. Most of the New Testament documents had been dated by Baur in the late second century. Was it possible in spite of Baur to fix the date beyond dispute at an earlier period? Lightfoot saw that the key to the problem lay with the two Apostolic Fathers, Clement and Ignatius, who were assigned by tradition to the period just before and after A.D. 100. If this traditional date were upheld, the New Testament must have fallen within the first century. That was why he followed up his work on Clement with an equally exhaustive study of Ignatius and Polycarp. This work was well advanced before he left Cambridge and was finally completed in his early years at Durham. It was published in three volumes in June 1885 and a second edition was called for in 1889. He then returned to his work on Clement, and two greatly enlarged volumes were brought out in 1890 shortly after his death. These five magnificent volumes on The Apostolic Fathers gave full scope to his gifts as an historian and set out all available information on the sub-apostolic age. Lightfoot had done just what he had set out to do; he had placed the date for the New Testament documents firmly in the context of the first Christian century. His work was hailed at once among English scholars as a knock-out for the Tübingen theory. Harnack declared that it was 'the greatest treatise of the century on patristic theology'.[154] C.K. Barrett described it as 'epoch making, and in a real sense, final'.[155] But there was more. It came into the hands of the dying Bishop Fraser, who read aloud to his Chaplain from the *Epistle of St Ignatius to The Ephesians* and then went on to say: 'Isn't it wonderful to think of Ignatius centuries ago cheering his friends at Ephesus with the same triumphant trust in Christ overcoming death that you and I have ourselves today?' The next morning he died. Lightfoot could hardly contain his emotion when he was told.[156]

Lightfoot's literary output never ceases to cause astonishment. His papers are housed in a cupboard in the Durham Cathedral Library, but they have never been properly sorted and indexed. In a letter dated November 28th 1983, Owen Chadwick told me: 'I once spent two days in a cold room in Durham, hunting through Lightfoot papers in packing cases.' His patristic studies ranged far beyond Ignatius and Polycarp, and he wrote numerous articles on individual Greek and Latin Fathers for the *Dictionary of Christian Biography.* The most outstanding of these articles was on Eusebius of Caesarea in the 1880 edition: 'the best and most exhaustive treatment of the life and writings of Eusebius' ever written.'[157] After his death, the Trustees of the Lightfoot Fund published six volumes of his sermons. Perhaps the most significant of these was the little volume entitled *Leaders in the Northern Church.* He was in fact 'among the first to claim for the Northumbrian mission of the seventh century its true position in the evangelization of England.'[158] But far the most valuable of these posthumous publications was the volume of *Biblical Essays* which appeared in 1893; and most valuable of all were the first three chapters of 198 pages on the 'Internal and External Evidence for the Authenticity and Genuineness of St John's Gospel'. The first chapter had been delivered as a lecture in 1871 and was printed in *The Expositor* in 1890. It seems that at one time he had thought of writing a Commentary on the Gospel, but 'happily', he said, 'it passed into other and better hands'.[159] Those hands were the hands of Westcott, whose great work on St John was first published as a volume in the *Speaker's Commentary* in 1880. Westcott's Introduction in support of the Johannine authorship soon became famous. But his arguments with their contracting circles were not original; they were drawn from Lightfoot. All that Westcott had to say had been said before, and said with far greater wealth of detail.

Lightfoot's mind was so well furnished that he could not have been better equipped for his chosen field of study.

He brought to all his work the sober judgment and perfect integrity of one whose heart was set on the pursuit of the *summum bonum*. Apart from his native English, he was at home in French and German, Spanish and Italian, Greek and Latin; and he had a working knowledge of Hebrew and Syriac, Arabic and Ethiopic. He was singled out by Dr Scrivener as one of three or four English scholars who were thoroughly acquainted with the Coptic dialects.[160] He was involved in the constant demands of a correspondence with professors, theologians, librarians and patristic scholars from all parts of Europe.[161] The first Appendix in *Lightfoot of Durham* prints a series of eight extracts from his letters to the Rev. J. Armitage Robinson between 1884 and 1888. They bear the marks of his 'incredible erudition'[162] and his scrupulous thoroughness as he sought to track down the most elusive quotations in the final stages of his work on Ignatius and Polycarp. So for example the first extract on May 19th 1884 reads as follows: 'Would you send me Pitra's Analecta Solesmensia Vol. II (I think it is Vol. II but possibly Vol. III) containing Saint Abercius. A large octavo vol. in paperback on the first shelf left hand above the ledge as you enter the anteroom to my study from the passage.'[163] But that task was easy compared with the later requests, and it says not a little for Armitage Robinson that he was able to comply. But even more remarkable was the perfect simplicity with which all his immense learning was clothed. Benson said that Lightfoot touched all classes with a simple appeal that was greater than his greatest volume.[164] And Moule said that what men recalled was his 'humanity with its gladness and its tears even more vividly than his immense knowledge, his masterly administration…and his literally life-breaking toil.'[165]

Archbishop Tait died in December 1882. There is some reason to believe that at one time Tait had thought of Lightfoot as his probable successor. Thus when Durham was under offer to Lightfoot, Church told Benson: 'All you urge is of the greatest weight...It is the point the Archbishop urged when Lightfoot saw him yesterday—and with good reason—though he frightened Lightfoot by expressing anxiety as to who there would be to take his own place if he were removed.'[166] But this did not eventuate since he had been so short a time in Durham, and the appointment fell to Benson, who had been Bishop of Truro since 1876. 'You will always be infinitely above and beyond me', Benson told Lightfoot on January 11th 1883, '... and I shall have ever the same reverence of and devotion to you.'[167] Two years later, on January 15th 1885, Benson wrote to Randall Davidson about the possible translation of Lightfoot from Durham to London: 'I do not wonder that you think J.B.L. would be the best counsellor for me. So he would, if he would counsel. But of late years his caution has grown upon him so exceedingly that I can get nothing out of him. 'I can't advise' has become a fixed phrase with him. The oldness of our friendship has made this rather a trial to me, and lately when he has been at Lambeth, it has been almost impossible to get him across the threshold from Lollards' Tower...Consequently all the opportunities for talk which are so essential were lost—and I got next to none. One wants to learn his view of things in casual ways, and not by direct interrogation always—for the latter fails, while it's of no use looking for the former...Hence I don't feel so sure that his sagacious perceptions, thorough consideration, and sound conclusions would have a fair chance of helping the Archbishopric work and counsel.'[168]

During the same January, Lightfoot himself wrote to Benson: 'No one can less regret than myself that I had not the offer of London. The wrench of leaving Durham would even be worse than the wrench which brought me here.'[169]

Lightfoot was quite unspoilt by the lure of personal ambition, and his work in Durham went on with as much vigour as ever. He had always abhorred party spirit, and controversies over ritualism were unheard of during his episcopate. He took an active part in the Convocation of York. He spoke four times at a Church Congress: Leicester in 1880; Newcastle in 1881; Carlisle in 1884; and Wolverhampton in 1887. He formed close links with the University of Durham, and in 1882 founded the De Bury Scholarship for men who were planning to take Orders in the Diocese. Then in 1887 he proposed to build a church for the people of Sunderland as a thank-offering for his seven years in Durham. The site chosen was in one of the most populous parts of the Diocese where the church would serve a working class parish of some ten thousand people. He was able to consecrate this new building, the Church of St Ignatius the Martyr, on July 2nd 1889, with one of the Sons of the House as the first incumbent. He refurnished the Chapel at Bishop Auckland and installed windows to depict the Northumbrian saints from Oswald and Aidan onwards. This work was finished while the Lambeth Conference was in session, and a distinguished company of some sixty Bishops from all parts of the Anglican Communion came for the Dedication on August 1st 1888. As for Lambeth, the fact that his lifelong friend Benson would preside was enough all else apart to engage his utmost cooperation. He was Chairman of the Committee on Purity and drafted its Report; but he did much more. Bishop Stubbs of Oxford said that 'in the leading part which he took in our deliberations, and by the authoritative wisdom, unwearied attention and elaborate work which were apparent in every word he said and every line he indited...(he) showed himself a very chief in counsel, pre-eminent in ability and service, as in learning and devotion.'[170]

What was Lightfoot's impact on that historic Diocese? Bishop Moule, who followed Westcott as Bishop of Durham. furnished an answer to that question in his sermon on 'Wise Men and Scribes' on December 10th 1907. 'Lightfoot', he said, 'still retains in the hearts of both clergy and people a place, not of honour only, but of love with which not even the splendour of Westcott's venerated name and more recent memory interferes.'[171] Bishop George Eden of Wakefield, preaching in Durham Cathedral on January 28th 1926, declared: 'Words are useless to convey any impression of the new life which sprang up in all directions under his inspiration and guidance. Vast schemes of Church extension seemed to grow up like magic; new Parishes, new Churches, Mission Districts, all alike were the fruit of his unstinted generosity and of the willing support of Churchmen. It is not too much to say, and as one who knew the Diocese before he came I dare to affirm it, that Bishop Lightfoot left a mark in the Diocese such as few, if any, before him had done.'[172] Moule and Eden had known Lightfoot intimately: Moule in Cambridge and Eden at Auckland Castle; but would the lapse of years and the rise of a new generation make a substantial difference in the way men thought of him? On the last day of the 1968 Lambeth Conference, I was among those who were asked to a buffet lunch at Lambeth. I was about to take the last place at one of the round tables when I heard the voice of Michael Ramsey telling me to come and sit down with him. I was on his left and another Archbishop was on his right. We knew that he had no small talk; conversation would be difficult. After one or two false starts, the meal went on in silence. Then I had a flash of inspiration. 'Your Grace', I said, 'while you were at Durham, was it possible at that distance in time still to trace the influence of Lightfoot and Westcott in the Diocese, and if that were the case, to say which of the two left the greater impact?' Like a shot, and with tremendous emphasis, he replied: 'Lightfoot!' And for the rest of the meal he went on to speak of Lightfoot with the utmost enthusiasm.

What was Lightfoot like as a man? There is universal testimony to the greatness of his mental stature and vast stores of learning; but what sort of person was he? Dean Farrar, an old friend and pupil, said of him within two months of his death: 'The facts of his inner life were revealed to few, perhaps fully to none.'[73] He was neither striking nor handsome in outward features and he had few social graces. He was shy and reserved, had no small talk, and made formal conversation with an effort; but when he broke into a smile, his face used to light up with a kind of glory. His own natural dignity was combined with perfect simplicity in a way that made an instant appeal to all classes, whether miners or magnates, clergy or people. No one knew him better in the hey-day of his episcopate than the Sons of the House; they came into daily contact with him in the intimacy of his home life. They knew him in moods of playful humour when he relaxed as well as in the most solemn moments of his Chapel sermons. But they loved and revered him in all moods alike, for they could not escape from the moral aura of his presence. His sons and his books went with him on his holiday excursions, and memories and anecdotes drawn from those days throw rays of light on his spirit. Once at Oban he went sailing and was caught in a squall which threatened to swamp the boat. He was quite unperturbed as he sat there with the manuscript of his work on Ignatius in hand. Or on another occasion while in Norway, he was calmly persevering with his proof-sheets while a small boy drove him down a rough and precipitous road to Romsdal Horn. The road was so narrow with a sheer drop on one side to the Lake below that his friends urged him to get out and walk. He looked over the edge and then replied: 'Other stolkjars must have taken this road. Drive on.' And he continued to correct the proof-sheets which had only arrived that morning.[174]

Lightfoot's friendship with Benson and Westcott was kept in repair by holidays together, generally in Scotland, often in Braemar. All three went to Braemar for the last time in September 1888 after the Lambeth Conference. It soon became clear that Lightfoot's health was seriously impaired. Overwork in his Diocese, topped off by his Lambeth labours, had led to a complete breakdown and the critical condition of his heart forced him to rest at Bournemouth for the winter. Benson went down to see him in November as soon as he had settled and found him in a nice house where he was on the mend: 'He can occupy himself for three-quarters of an hour at a time with light literary work, and frequently does.'[175] Benson went down to Bournemouth again in February 1889 and wrote with some surprise: 'Dunelm strangely better, colour, expression, brightness, all trickling back to life…He said with tears, 'I want to tell you how good God has been to me in this illness—I have had so many happinesses—seeds I had sown have been coming up in the diocese so fast; long before I looked for it.'[176] Lightfoot was able to return home in May, and Benson wrote to him in July: 'One line tonight to express the solemn, almost trembling, joy with which I learn from letter after letter that your strength is your own again.'[177] The Diocesan Conference was held in October. 'He came slowly walking up the aisle. The Conference stood listening to his weary footfall.'[178] It was his last Presidential Address. He suffered a relapse and went back to Bournemouth on December 3rd. 'His passion for work never left him,'[179] and on December 18th, the last words that he wrote were to add a sentence to his work on Clement while the doctor was out of the room. For the next two days he was drifting in and out of consciousness; and on St Thomas' Day, December 21st, he died from heart trouble with its complications. Benson was at once advised. 'A telegram from Eden at Bournemouth that my dearest and oldest friend passed away peacefully at 3.45 this afternoon.'[180]

A memorial service was held in Durham Cathedral on the morning of December 27th in the presence of a vast congregation drawn from 'all classes and all corners of the Diocese and of England'.[181] Lightfoot's body was then taken by road to Auckland Castle and laid to rest under the east end of the central aisle in the Chapel. Benson stood at the foot of the grave and read the words of committal while Westcott stood at the head and cast the earth over his body. And Hort was there as well. They could hardly measure the depth of their feeling or the sense of their loss; but while they stood on the brink of eternity, they knew that such love was stronger than death.[182] Lightfoot had been the central figure in that remarkable group of men. He was not a mystic like Westcott, nor a philosopher-theologian like Hort, nor a lover of ceremonial like Benson. 'He had little love of symbolism or elaborate forms in worship.'[183] His sympathies and convictions were most neatly summed up in his own words: 'Not Augustine, but Aidan, is the true Apostle of England.'[184]

One short postscript may be added. The Bishop of Salisbury, John Wordsworth, was at dinner with a group of Ordinands on St Thomas' Day in 1889 when a telegram was brought in and handed to him. His face went white as he read it; he rose from the table in great distress, excused himself and left the room. It was only later that the Ordinands were told that the telegram had brought him news of the death of Lightfoot. One of them at least never forgot the look of grief on Wordsworth's face as he absorbed the news. Thirty-three years later, on St Thomas' Day 1922, his son was to kneel on Lightfoot's grave at the foot of the Sanctuary steps in the Chapel at Auckland Castle for ordination as a Deacon. That was Philip Nigel Warrington Strong, who was to become the great war-time Bishop of New Guinea and later the Archbishop of Brisbane and Primate of Australia. Philip Strong always felt that his father's ordination on the day of Lightfoot's death and his own ordination kneeling on Lightfoot's grave had brought him a touch of Lightfoot's spirit.

For Further Reading

F.J.A. Hort: *J.B. Lightfoot* (Article in Dictionary of National Biography), 1892.

H.W. Watkins *J.B. Lightfoot* (article in Quarterly Review), 1893.

H.C.G. Moule: *Wise Men and Scribes,* 1907.

H.C.G. Moule: *My Cambridge Classical Teachers,* 1913.

G.E. Eden & F.C. Macdonald: *Lightfoot of Durham,* 1932.

Stephen Neill: *Interpretation of the New Testament, 1861-1961,* 1964.

C.K. Barrett: *Joseph Barber Lightfoot,* Durham University Journal, Vol. LXIV3, 1972.

J.A.T. Robinson: *Joseph Barber Lightfoot* (Durham Cathedral, 1981.

A.F. Benson: *Life of Edward White Benson,* 1899.

David Newsome: *Godliness and Good Learning.*

Randall Davidson: *The Life of Archibald Campbell Tait.*

Appendix

Elizabeth Clephane
and
Her Hymns

A centuries-old Abbey, now in ruins, looks down on the little border town of Melrose and casts an aura of old-fashioned romance over its quiet streets and houses. The mantle of history and tradition wraps itself round the village as it reaches far back into by-gone ages. It was Aidan of Lindisfarne who established the first religious foundation in what is now called Old Melrose, two miles to the east of the present site. This was meant to be a daughter of the monastic house of Lindisfarne and its first two Priors were St Boisil and St Cuthbert. It was from this centre that the gospel began to spread along the Scottish borders; it stood like a light on the hill until it was destroyed in 839 A.D. Three hundred years were to pass; then in 1136 David I asked the Cistercian monks from Rievaulx Abbey in

North Yorkshire to found a new Abbey below the Eildon Hills. The east end of the Abbey was dedicated in 1146; other buildings were added in the years that followed. For the next four hundred years it stood to serve the border people of Scotland, but at length it crumbled into ruins some time after 1660. Within its precincts, the heart of Robert the Bruce, embalmed and encased in lead, was laid to rest. Clustered round its vast south gate, the little town of Melrose grew up. Today, it is described as a charming village of some 1500 people, nestling in the upper valley of the Tweed between Galashiels and Kelso. Its central feature is a classic market square with its Memorial to St Boswell; that is, to St Boisil, the first Prior. The houses round the Square and in the background have weathered many a bleak winter. And it was at Bridgend House that Elizabeth Cecilia Douglas Clephane died in 1869.

I well remember a cold Saturday afternoon in February 1950 when I was driven through the little town of Melrose. As we passed a row of houses, one of them was pointed out to me as the erstwhile home of Elizabeth Clephane. I can not be certain, but I think there was a plaque to record the fact. Elizabeth Clephane was born in Edinburgh on 18th June 1830, but spent most of her life in Melrose. Her life story can now only be told in bare detail, but her father, Andrew Clephane, was the County Sheriff for Fife and Kinross. Elizabeth was the youngest of four children; she had to look up to her two sisters and a brother. She was always frail and often unwell, and she never married. But from her girlhood years, she was a well-taught and devoted Christian, and she wore herself out in her care for the poor and needy. She gave away all her money, even selling a horse and carriage of sorts so that she might have more to give. She was always bright and cheerful, always welcome in the homes of the poor who liked to call her 'the Sunbeam of Melrose'. She poured out her heart in private through the hymns which she composed as poems, but they were meant only for her own eyes. After her death on 19th February 1869 at the early age of thirty-eight, her poems were found locked in her desk. In due course, eight of them were published in 1872 in *The Family Treasury*. This was a Scottish Presbyterian Magazine, and the hymns or poems were then copied in *The Christian Age* in 1874. It was an age when hymn singing was still a new thing in the Church of Scotland, but two of her poems, the first and the last, were to become much loved hymns in most English Hymnals.

The first of the eight was the hymn 'Beneath the cross of Jesus I fain would take my stand'. It was apparently written in 1868 within a year of her death and it should always be sung to the tune of St Christopher. It was written as a poem to be pondered in the silence of her own soul when her eye at times could see the very dying form of Him Who had suffered there for her; but it is a very moving hymn when sung with reverence and humility. It is steeped in imagery drawn from both the Old and the New Testament and it is an intensely personal expression of trust and worship. There are four stanzas, each with eight lines: the first four lines are a statement of some aspect of fact or truth; the next four lines are the response of an adoring worshipper. The hymn does not try to describe the Cross itself: there is scarcely more than a hint of the physical pain and suffering of the Passion. It does not try to melt the heart through a vivid picture of One Whose face was marred with pain and sorrow, but hearts are touched far more effectively by its wistful way of sensitive allusion. The language is chaste, the emotion is controlled, and the onward rhythm of the words matches the rising swell of devotion. It is a noble hymn that leads one to kneel afresh in spirit at the foot of the Cross and to worship the Son of God Who loved us and gave Himself for us.

> O Christ, beneath that shadow
> Be my abiding place;
> I ask no other sunshine than
> The sunshine of Thy face.

Undoubtedly the best known and most loved of all Passion hymns is that of Isaac Watts: 'When I survey the wondrous Cross on which the Prince of Glory died'. There may well be room for debate as to which hymn should stand second, but there is much to be said in favour of that of Elizabeth Clephane. It is interesting to trace ways in which they relate to each other. They are equally reverent, dignified and profound in worship; they share the same delicate touch in allusion to the physical elements of the Passion. Isaac Watts has never been excelled in plain Anglo-Saxon language with words of monosyllabic strength and simplicity. This is seen in the most luminous and telling effect in the stanza.

> See from His head, His hands, His feet
> Sorrow and love flow mingled down:
> Did e'er such love and sorrow meet,
> Or thorns compose so rich a crown.

Elizabeth Clephane's language came from the heart; it was more intimate, more personal, more revealing of the love that held her spell-bound at the foot of the Cross. It was as though her eyes looked into His eyes, and the word that His eyes spelt was that word love. She knew herself to be sinful, lost, and undone; she could not look into those eyes and plead any claim of her own. But His was a love that reached down to meet her in all her need and just where she was.

> And from my stricken heart with tears
> Two wonders I confess:
> The wonders of His glorious love
> And my own worthlessness.

The last in the series of eight poems published in *The Family Treasury* was the hymn commonly known as 'The Ninety and Nine'. Julian's great Dictionary says that it was 'probably written in 1868'. It seems far more probable that it was written many years before when it grew out of deep sorrow as the result of a tragic family bereavement.[185] Elizabeth's elder brother George had failed to make good at home and had been sent out to Canada to live on a monthly remittance from his father. He had only drifted further into trouble and his allowance was wasted on alcohol. One night in May 1851 he was so drunk that he could not walk back to his lodgings. He had fallen down, could not get up, and lay on the road until he was found in the morning. He was carried into the home of a friendly doctor under whose roof he died from the effects of alcohol and exposure. He was buried in the grave yard of St Andrew's Church in Fergus, Ontario. When the news of his death reached his home in Melrose, the whole family felt its pain and sorrow; but none more than Elizabeth who was then not quite twenty one years old. She went into her room and closed the door to be alone with that sore grief. She had loved her wayward brother and could not but believe that God had loved him too. Perhaps even in his dying moments, he had mercy sought and mercy found. She took a piece of paper and slowly found an outlet for her feelings. Then she locked it in her desk and it did not see the light of day until after her death. What was it that she wrote?

> There were ninety and nine that safely lay
> In the shelter of the fold:
> But one was out on the hills away,
> Far off from the gates of gold:
> Away on the mountains wild and bare,
> Away from the tender Shepherd's care.

But there was more to tell. In February 1874, Moody and Sankey came to Glasgow where Moody was the guest of the great Scottish preacher Andrew Bonar. They left Glasgow at length on May 20th for two days of special meetings in Edinburgh.[186] Just before they boarded the train, Sankey bought a copy of *The Christian Age*, a small penny weekly. He scanned it in the train in the hope that he would find some news of America, but he was disappointed and put it down. The train was not far from Edinburgh when he picked it up again and caught sight of Elizabeth Clephane's little poem. He read it to Moody, but Moody was absorbed in his correspondence and did not hear a word. Sankey cut it out and placed it in his scrap book, but then thought no more of it. But in Edinburgh there was a great meeting when Moody was in the chair and Horatius Bonar gave a short but moving address on The Good Shepherd. Moody turned to Sankey and asked him to sing something appropriate. Sankey could think of nothing except the hymn he had read in the train. But it was not set to music, and he had no new music that would fit; yet there was no escape from the feeling that this was what he had to sing. He took out the cutting and placed it on the harmonium. Then he struck the note of A flat, and began. Note by note the tune came; verse by verse it remained the same, and this was the form it has held ever since. And as the last words were sung, a great sigh went up from that congregation. Moody himself had seldom felt so moved; there were tears in his eyes as he raised his hand and pronounced the Benediction. But God alone saw the link between that quiet grave in Ontario and the spiritual harvest to be reaped in Scotland.

There can be no doubt who was in Elizabeth's mind as she wrote of the sheep that was 'away on the mountains wild and bare', and the plight of that sheep is seen in the details of drama and danger that marked the search. But the primary emphasis falls on the Good Shepherd rather than the Lost Sheep. The hymn drew a vivid picture by the imaginative use of Old Testament language and imagery and the details of the search are all stamped on the screen of our mind. But that was all lifted up to a superlative level as the hymn was sung by Sankey. Let the words of J.C. Pollock sum it all up: 'As the impromptu melody, pibroch-like, redolent of moor and mist, rose little by little in pitch and tension to its peak in the fifth line falling right back in half the last-line to point rest, every man and woman saw the Good Shepherd leave the ninety and nine, climb the rough road, cross the deep waters and thorn thickets, the storm-racked mountain to find His one lost sheep, sick and helpless, and ready to die.'[187] That hymn! Sung to that tune! Who could resist its moving appeal? Who could escape its haunting beauty? It was not just that the shepherd's search was described in unforgettable language. The spiritual impact was greater by far. Elizabeth Clephane's own heart-broken sorrow was a revelation of the wonderful tenderness in the heart of the Good Shepherd for all who are lost and out of the way.

> And all through the mountains, thunder riven,
> And up from the rocky steep,
> There rose a cry to the gate of heaven
> Rejoice! I have found My sheep!
> And the angels echoed round the throne.
> Rejoice! For the Lord brings back His own!

Let no one miss the sheer exultation in the last line of that hymn. There is joy in the presence of the angels of God when the Lord brings back one of His own. This was the high note of a hymn that would sweep through the churches in the late Victorian era. But that shy and gentle woman never knew how her hymn would come to be held in honour. She had composed her hymns for the solace of her own soul; she drew all her comfort from faith in the Lord Jesus. She thought of Him as the Saviour Who had died for her on the Cross; she looked to Him as the Shepherd Whose heart went out to the last and the least. She lived in the hearts of the poor and needy; it was her joy to be thought of as 'the Sunbeam of Melrose'. The key to this sunny spirit lay in her deep personal devotion to Christ the Lord. This was the great motivating force in her life. There might well have been an echo in her own heart of the words of St Paul: 'What things were gain to me, those I counted loss for Christ' (Ph. 3:7). It is surely significant that the burden of this text left its mark on both Isaac Watts and Elizabeth Clephane in their hymns on the Cross. Isaac Watts had written with an air of measured solemnity:

> When I survey the wondrous Cross
> On which the Prince of Glory died,
> My richest gain I count but loss,
> And pour contempt on all my pride.

What could have been finer than that! In sentiment and expression alike, it was nearly perfect. Elizabeth's approach was perhaps more gentle, but just as telling as a revelation of her own heart:

> Content to let the world go by,
> And count its gain but loss,
> This sinful self my only shame,
> My only hope the Cross.

For Further Reading

Julian, *The Evangelical Christian,* 1940

John Pollock: *D. L. Moody : Moody Without Sankey,* (Christian Focus Publications 2005).

Endnotes

1 J.B. Lightfoot, *Leaders of the Northern Church*, (1890), 41.
2 Bishop Westcott, in Lightfoot, 178.
3 Lightfoot, 33.
4 William Bright, *Chapters of Early English Church History* (1877), 152–3.
5 Bright, 155.
6 Lightfoot, 43.
7 Lightfoot, 8.
8 Bright, 178.
9 Bright, 176.
10 Bright, 185.
11 Lightfoot, 44.
12 Lightfoot, 44.
13 Lightfoot, 31.
14 Bright, 164.
15 Lightfoot, 9.
16 Bright, 211.
17 Lightfoot, 50.
18 Bright, 231.
19 Bright, 244.
20 Bright, 239.
21 Bright, 306.
22 Bright, 375.
23 Bright, 378.
24 Lightfoot, 78.
25 Lightfoot, 14.
26 G.M. Trevelyan, *England in The Age of Wycliffe* (1899), 80.
27 Margaret Deansley, *The Lollard Bible* (1920), 225.
28 Trevelyan, 42.
29 Trevelyan, 128.
30 Trevelyan, 306.
31 Deansley, 229.
32 Deansley, 239.
33 Deansley, 241.
34 Deansley, 258–9.
35 Trevelyan, 142.
36 Deansley, 234.
37 Deansley, 234.
38 Deansley, 259.
39 Deansley, 234.
40 Deansley, 234.

41 Trevelyan, 311.

42 Trevelyan, 319.

43 Trevelyan, 335.

44 Trevelyan, 335.

45 Trevelyan, 335.

46 Deansley, 278–9.

47 Trevelyan, 350.

48 John Foxe, vol.IV, 635.

49 Foxe, vol. IV, 635.

50 Seebohm, 399.

51 Foxe, vol. IV, 638.

52 Foxe, vol. IV, 638.

53 Foxe, vol. IV, 635; cf. p.633.

54 Foxe, vol. IV, 635.

55 Thomas Becon: The Catechism and other pieces (Parker Society), 426.

56 Foxe, vol. IV, 656.

57 Foxe, vol. VII, 138.

58 Hugh Latimer, Sermons, 334.

59 Latimer: Sermons, 834.

60 Foxe, vol. VII, 452.

61 Cranmer, vol. II, 344.

62 Ibid, 345–6.

63 McCulloch: Thomas Cranmer, 360.

64 Whitefield: Twenty Five Sermons (1740) Sermon xxii, 775.

65 A Short Account, 44.

66 Whitefield: Seventy Five Sermons; Sermon LXXIII, 767.

67 Whitefield: Works Vol. II, Letter DCXXII, 127.

68 Works: vol. III, Letter CCLXXV, 14.

69 John Gillies: *The Life of The Rev. George Whitefield*, 265.

70 J.C. Ryle: *Christian Leaders of the Last Century*, 50–57.

71 *The Life and Times of the Countess of Huntingdon*, vol. I, 92.

72 A.R. Buckland: Selected Sermons of George Whitefield, Introduction, xvi.

73 *The Life and Times of Selina, Countess of Huntingdon*, vol. I, 92.

74 Tyerman: *The Life of The Rev. George Whitefield*, vol. II, 596.

75 Ibid, vol. II, 598.

76 G.O. Trevelyan: *The Life and Letters of Lord Macauley*, 509. ?? (Silver Library, one vol. ed. 1908)

77 H.B. Liddon: *Life of Edward Bouverie Pusey* [1894], Vol.1, 255

78 Norman Wymer: *Dr Arnold of Rugby*, 136.

79 Standish Meacham: *Lord Bishop, The Life of Samuel Wilberforce*, 15.

80 Ibid, 61.

81 J.L. and Barbara Hammond: *Lord Shaftesbury*, 251.

82 *A.E. Benson: The Life of Edward White Benson*, vol. II, 12.

83 cf. G.R. Ballein: *History of The Evangelical Party*, 227.

84 G.K.A. Bell: *Randall Davidson*, vol. II, 1242.

85 G.E. Eden and F.C. Macdonald (eds), *Lightfoot of Durham*, 149.

86 I have not seen this article or booklet.

87 J.A.T. Robinson, 6.

88 *Lightfoot of Durham*, 1.

89 Ibid, 147.

90 A.C. Benson, *The Life of Edward White Benson*, vol.1, 26.

91 David Newsome, *Godliness and Good Learning*, 113.

92 F.J.A. Hort, in *Dictionary of National Biography*.

93 Benson, vol.1, 40.

94 Ibid, vol.1, 324.

95 Hort, in D.N.B.

96 *Lightfoot of Durham*, 3.

97 Benson, vol.2, 819.

98 *Lightfoot of Durham*, 3 footnote.

99 Hort, in D.N.B.

100 Benson, vol.1, 55.

101 Ibid, vol.1, 74–5.

102 C.K. Barrett, "Joseph Barber Lightfoot" (in the Durham University Journal, vol.LXIV3, June 1972), 194.

103 C.K. Barrett, 193.

104 *Lightfoot of Durham*, 150.

105 Benson, vol.1, 121.

106 Ibid, vol.1, 56.

107 Randall Davidson, *The Life of Archibald Campbell Tait*, vol.1, 207.

108 Ibid, vol.1, 537.

109 H.C.G. Moule, "My Cambridge Classical Teachers", 13.

110 Ibid, 13.

111 H.C.G. Moule, "Wise Men and Scribes" (in *Cathedral and University and Other Sermons*), 13.

112 H.C.G. Moule, "My Cambridge Classical Teachers", 13; "Wise Men and Scribes", 13.

113 *Lightfoot of Durham*, 4 footnote 1.

114 Ibid, 150.

115 Ibid, 124.

116 J.B. Lightfoot, Preface to *Galatians*, viii.

117 cf. J.A.T. Robinson, 6.

118 Lightfoot, *Galatians*, vii.

119 cf. *Lightfoot of Durham*, 129.

120 Stephen Neill: *The Interpretation of the New Testament*, 1861–1961, 38.

121 cf. *Lightfoot of Durham*, 131.

122 Benson, vol.2, 9.

123 Ibid, vol.1, 196.

124 Benson, vol.1, p,231.

125 Ibid, vol.1, 258. But for an alternative account, see A.C. Benson, *Leaves of the Tree*, quoted by Robinson, 4.

126 Ibid, vol.1, 258.

127 Ibid., vol.1, 314.

128 J.A.T. Robinson, 11.

129 J.B. Harford and F.C.

Macdonald, *Handley Carr Glynn Moule*, 299.

[130] Randall Davidson, vol.2, 132.

[131] *Lightfoot of Durham*, 178.

[132] Ibid, 10.

[133] Ibid, 11.

[134] Hort, in *D.N.B.*

[135] *Lightfoot of Durham*, 83.

[136] Lightfoot, *Ordination Addresses*, 217–18.

[137] Stephen Neill, 37.

[138] C.K. Barrett, 196.

[139] C.K. Barrett, 197.

[140] Stephen Neill, 37.

[141] *Lightfoot of Durham* p.15.

[142] Ibid, 32.

[143] Ibid, 20.

[144] Randall Davidson, vol.2, 517.

[145] *Lightfoot of Durham*, 58.

[146] Benson, vol.1, 499.

[147] *Lightfoot of Durham*, xiv.

[148] *Lightfoot of Durham*, 96.

[149] Ibid, 49.

[150] Ibid, xi.

[151] *Lightfoot of Durham*, 107–8.

[152] Prefatory Note to *The Apostolic Fathers, Part 1, S. Clement of Rome*, vii.

[153] Introductory Note to *Biblical Essays*, vi.

[154] Stephen Neill, 57.

[155] C.K. Barrett, 195.

[156] *Lightfoot of Durham*, 57.

[157] *Lightfoot of Durham*, 180.

[158] Ibid, 111.

[159] *Biblical Essays*, 1.

[160] *Lightfoot of Durham*, 119.

[161] Ibid, 117.

[162] J.A.T. Robinson, 12.

[163] *Lightfoot of Durham*, 161.

[164] Benson, vol.2, 291.

[165] H.C.G. Moule, "Wise Men and Scribes", 10–11.

[166] Cf. *Lightfoot of Durham*, 12.

[167] Benson, vol.1, 560.

[168] Randall Davidson, vol.1, 169.

[169] Benson. vol.2, 46.

[170] *Lightfoot of Durham*, 74.

[171] H.C.G. Moule, "Wise Men and Scribes", 10.

[172] *Lightfoot of Durham*, xv.

[173] Cf. J.A.T. Robinson. p.7.

[174] *Lightfoot of Durham*, 45.

[175] Benson, vol.2, 228.

[176] Benson, vol.2, 255.

[177] Ibid, vol.2, 264.

[178] *Lightfoot of Durham*, 75.

[179] Ibid, 99.

[180] Benson, vol.2, 290.

[181] *Lightfoot of Durham* p.101.

[182] Ibid, 102.

[183] *Lightfoot of Durham*, 158.

[184] Lightfoot, *Leaders in the Northern Church*, 9.

[185] cf. The Evangelical Christian, November 1940.

[186] Cf. J.C. Pollock, *Moody Without Sankey*, 121–3.

[187] J.C. Pollock: *Moody Without Sankey*, 122–3.